Poems Ruled
by the Heart

*To Sharon
John's Book*

Poems Ruled by the Heart

*love
MUM*

John Edward Johnson

Copyright © 2012 by John Edward Johnson.

Library of Congress Control Number: 2012905718
ISBN: Hardcover   978-1-4691-9146-1
               Softcover   978-1-4691-9145-4
               Ebook   978-1-4691-9147-8

All rights reserved. No part of this book may be reproduced or transmitted in any form or by any means, electronic or mechanical, including photocopying, recording, or by any information storage and retrieval system, without permission in writing from the copyright owner.

This book was printed in the United States of America.

To order additional copies of this book, contact:
Xlibris Corporation
0-800-644-6988
www.xlibrispublishing.co.uk
Orders@xlibrispublishing.co.uk
303288

These poems are extracted from letters sent over a period of forty-two years—a very strong and emotional love affair.

Included:

    a poem of his friend, an airman
        a poem of his father, written when his father passed away
        a poem when I had his son.

Remembering Gravelly Hollow

When the breath of twilight
Blows flame to misty skies
All its vaporous sapphire violet glow
And the silver moon and silver gleams
With their magic, flood through us two
And through the gateway of thy eyes
We are one with twilight dreams
When trees and skies are in surly mood
And my heart is wrapped around thy breast
Full of peace and sleep and dreams
In this vast quietude we are one with our hearts at rest
Then from our joys of countryside and love
We stray along the margin of the unknown tide
With all its reach of soundless calm
The lips above all can thrill me far beyond any flirtation with life
Aye and deep, deep, and deeper let me drink
And draw from thou fountain more light, more peace with awe
Our two hearts growing as one with our silent dreams

Beloved I hath given thee my very soul,
For hath not we two dwelt in paradise,
Then let life be so simple,
We would contemplate whole days on some thought,
Frail as a white snowdrop,
We desired the earth and found beauty, in one another,
Beloved, let us continue as children of the earth,
Amongst the simple flowers, for a little while,
The tall bluebells, violets, and snowdrops,
They fill our very night with perfume,
Let us remain with silent eyes,
Not fearing, scarce perceiving, to ourselves,
Complete in one another until the end,
Let us stand silent together, silent still,
Against some tree, within the trunk,
Thus let us pass back to the everlasting,
Out of which we came; we have, beloved,
These few seasons dwelt, together with the flowers of paradise,

On Arnot Hill Road, on a summer's day, I met her first and knew,
That her dark hair would weave a snare that one day I might rue, (never)
I saw the danger, yet I walked along the enchanted way,
And said, let grief be a fallen leaf at dawning of the day,
On Sandfield Road in November, we tripped lightly along the ledge,
Of a deep ravine where could be seen the bond of passion's pledge,
The queen of my heart, still baking tarts and I not making hay,
O! I loved too much, and by such, such happiness is thrown away,
I gave her gifts of mind; I gave her the secret sign,
Of word of tint, I gave her poems to say,
With her own name there and her own dark hair, like clouds over the fields of May,
Yet though time hast past do I still not see,
In the quiet gentle rain of Burntstump Plantation,
Where old ghosts meet, I see her walking now,
Wouldst that I had not wooed her as a creature of clay,
For I lost my love at the dawn of day.

Country Love

When we two meet, in some Arnold noisy street,
And the atmosphere heavy with grimed air,
Red orange with harsh electric glare from blatant neon signs,
When chimney pots seem lines of dwarfed and crooked men,
And thoughts likewise are twisted, then my heart begins to beat,
To that rhythmic sound of pattering feet,
That hurry and surge around us two, and I feel lit with a quickening glow,
That gailey we tread along life's path, hours are moments,
For I am so in love with you.

But with thee, oh, this country love,
'tis different; here the sky is so blue above,
And the silence so profound,
That one can hear unseen animals walking through the grass,
The trees that sway and tremble in the afternoon breeze,
As we two lay upon grassy ground,
Soft and tender beneath our world of love,
What I wonder could be more sweet than this moment,
Than to be by thy side and admire this view,
Our other life and world it matters not,
The world's dusty glows soon forgot,
In our contentment, content to be with each other,
For I am so in love with you.

Before I fall silent finally,
I want to make one last attempt,
And tell of my absurd desire to compose,
For thee, one single poem, with my mental eyes, wide open,
And without even one lapse,
From that most scrupulous truth which I pursue,
Of this love we both hast known,
Running through our years,
Perhaps only the poem I can never write,
Is of us two.

The small times count
The inches and the miles
Touches not traditions
These will fill our senses, our memories
In the morning or in the end
Life should not be lived in steps
That lead from year to year
Or even day to decade
Only moment to moment
Love to love

One more breath from thee against my own
Might have brought the loss of innocence
Yet to have lost love, never to smile again,
For after coming up through almost fifty years
I was but a breath away from a new life
But innocent I am and will remain
Of thy body melting into mine

Some words come too late to matter
A phone call never made
A letter put away lost, unanswered
We lose a chapter another chance
Because of hesitation
Words flow easily
How have we two come this far together?
How do we go on without each other?

Are flowers the winter choice?
Is love's bed always snow,
And love's appeal to know?
I never saw a sweeter face
As thine; I know as I stand before
My heart has left its dwelling place
And can return no more

Love was born in an instant
Involuntarily torn, from this my lonely heart
At thy first glance I knew thee ever
How strange, never did I know
That love was like this
To lose thee now would be such a loss
Parted from thee I am desolate

Your chiselled lips, your lovely golden head
Were fairer than the petals of a flower
And on the shaven surface of the lawn
You moved like music. And smiled like dawn
The leaves, the flowers, the dragonflies, the dew
The radiant glory of a summer do
Were all part of the wonder that was you

Hand in hand we will walk this land
Until journey's end
I know not what lies beyond
Be it nothingness or a new dawn
But with thee I shall rejoice
For my choice is with thee
The tenderness of thy touch
Never ceases to move me so much
There's evermore than there's to behold
Such bliss, happiness, and joy untold
For thee, my love, are beyond compare

I wish nothing more now
Except to stay here spent, even on this day
These arms, thy arms, the road's end
And thy tired face, tired face
Already reaching into sleep
The climax of the climax
Taking time out to love
Is what it is all about

From our joys of countryside and love
We strayed along the margin of the unknown tide
All this soundless calm, thy word, thy lips
Thee above can thrill me, far beyond any flirtation with life
Full of peace, sleep, and dreams in this vast quietude
We are one with our hearts at rest

Remembering how thee ever gave thy love to me
Now, when I feel my courage flicker low,
Thy spirit comes to breathe it into flames
Until I lift my head and smiling go
Whispering softly thy beloved name
And from out of the shadows thee watch
Lest I should weep

Thee, who I gladly walk with, touch
Or wait for as one certain of good
We know, we know that this love needs
More than the admiring excitement of union
More than the abrupt self-confident farewell.
Are we not seekers of happiness,
All who follow the simple wish?
It's later than you think, nearer the day
Amid the stirring of the trees and lovers' sighs
We escape; this time, however short, is ours

Of being young again, happiness is endless
I know this paradise, that all hast dreamt of all their lives
And beyond these trees, beyond the deep blue air
North is nowhere and is endless
Ye how I wish we were starting through life at the very beginning
The trees and dark bushes are not so arrogant as they were
Nor is thy lover as when he is alone
Yet what is this sadness and longing that comes over me
As thy face touches mine
My love, thee art my love

But we will walk upon the wooded hill
Of Burntstump Plantation
Where stands a grove, of birch, of pine
Where the downy twilight droops her wing
And no waters glimmer
Our hearts shall listen still
For pines gossip the whole wood through
Tell full of their runtic tales to sigh and sift
'tis ever sweet to be with thee
And though the fanciful rabbits stir
And windy odours light as thistledown
Breathe from the runtic pine
We forget our wandering and pain
Half remembering days that hast gone
We dream a dream that we are home again
Dreaming the great dreams of youth
And saying no word of love, we look into each other
And find that we dream as one

Do not hurry spring
The wind still trembles in empty trees
And dead geraniums stand still
Another week perhaps, when skaters leave the pond
And now for a while longer
We can have the river bank to ourselves
I need a little while longer with thee now
There are many things about us two
I do not know
Do thee like my day-to-day character?
Do I worry thee when I frown?
Where were thee when I was growing up?
Distance breaks not the ties of love
Lovers are lovers evermore
By the light and into the darkness
Thy fragrant rose will grow beyond the wall
We sleep together in nobody's world
But our own—a quiet sleep
A stomach-to-stomach sleep
That wraps us in each

Autumn: Burntstump Park

Autumn is upon us now as we lie, beneath creamy clouds of latticed light,
That hint of darkness but descry a rosy flicker through the night,
The ways are gold with the leaves Autumn blows about the air,
The trees sing anthems of despair, thee my Love bind the sheaves,
Of thy raven hair more softly and weave more subtly bars of a song,
That bear bright children of love debonair, and laughter lightly comes and reaves,
The garland from our sorrow's brow, life rises up, joy fills our cup,
That flashes clear, the year fades in a whisper now, shadow and silence now my throne
The seasons—we were happy here, 'tis autumn and the dying breeze,
Murmurs 'Embrace'; the moon replies, 'Embrace' the soughing of the trees,
Calls us to linger loverwise and drain our passion to the lees,
'tis autumn, the belated dove calls through the beeches that bestir,
Themselves to kiss the skies above, as I kiss thee,
Leave us, sweet autumn, to our love. Thy Jonathan (with love)

The Letter

Coming to write my last letter to thee in this year 1975
I am happy, yet I am sad
I think of others passing as they have passed
So many days of sun that never shone
Letters and days, and this is not the last
I must doubt to see them stretching on
And I must wonder if it would be strange
Sooner or later for our love to change
And yet I know our love has won the toss
So many times, and most of that day
When thee first said 'yes, we will meet'
One word I was half-afraid to say
What I felt suddenly in dread of loss
And then thee came my way
Thy smile as thee panted up the hill, could only be a sign
And now it all comes back, to breathe, to live, and to shine
And so I run through how our love began
This encounter, while we hardly thought
And pleasant company without a plan
But then the wild desire, and we were caught
How then we were afraid and blight and ban
Clawed we two, like devils, but we fought
And in the end won sweetness from it all
And how it would be sweeter to recall
And surely we will call it up again, and laugh and sing
Knowing it is not a dream, but plain and true
We shall never find a better thing

Then we two shall bless but plain and true
We shall never ever find a better thing
Then we two shall bless, what we have bought with pain
And close it like two halves of a ring
But now I only tell my letter go
And say my darling I love you so

Sweet closes the eve on Burntstump Wood
And blithely awakens tomorrow
But the pride of spring in this wood
Can yield nothing but sorrow
I see the spreading leaves and flowers
I hear the wild birds singing
But pleasure they have none for me
Whilst with care my heart is wringing

Oh, to see thee laugh again
That unmistaken sparkle of love in thine eye
I live again. It's joy, it's wealth, it's life itself
Thy lover prays above all
That love, happiness, health
Will always be thine
We emerge from the darkness
The bond betwixt us two
Is stronger than ever

Fragments of thy rich imagining
Splinter and echo within
My heart lifts to the beating of thine
Strung to the pitch of thy demanding beauty
I am resonant to no other touch
That sets my spirit soaring

For this I hold
Friendship is more than life
Longer than love
It shall prove worthier to the spirit

When the body is cold
There is no wisdom that can reach
Truth, if truth can no answer give
The deepest sorrow cannot teach
Thee, my love, how to live

Be gentle with me, new love
Treat me tenderly
I need a gentle touch
Thy soft voice
The candlelight after nine
There have been so many
Who did not understand
Nor did they want to know
So give me all the love that I see
In those timid brown eyes
But give it gently

Once more I hear the music of the lark
Piping clear and shrill
Oh, there it is again
Trilling as sweetly still
Once more I hear the softness of thy voice
Above the thunder of despair
Confusion. Doubt and folly pass
Leaving our love still fair
Forever will I hear the lark
And still see thee gathering
Roses in the dark

Eternity is life, when love has gone
There is no sunset and no dawn
Only the dear monotonous grey
Of some interminable day

Sweet one, I love thee for thy lovely shape
For the art of loving thee make
In love in bed in rhymes
But most because we see into each other's minds
There to read secrets and to trust
And to cancel time

Love is not ours to command or commend
But a wreath of fulfilment offering we two
Ourselves through the gift of surrender
Not to be lightly taken ever but made at home
Love, because of the tears and our human needs
Rehearses death in desiring all the fears
Till love unlocks its tethered floods

The way thee bring thy lover to ecstasy
Despite my pride, ignorance, and exhaustion
Yet thee, my love, are satisfied, and so was I this night
Thee never fail to show me
A beautiful morning from every night
And return me to living my youngest years
Thus I watch thee in thy dream
Whilst the blue night creeps upon us

If ever I saw a blessing in the air, I see it now
For thee are in my arms, contented and without care
Here in our lane of happiness
Where brown and green of fields and hedges drip
Through golden sunlight on the powder of my eye
When all the world sweats with beads of spring upon its bud
If ever I heard a blessing, it is here
Where birds in the tree splash with hidden wings
Drops of sound break on my ears
I know that if ever lovers were blessed, it is now

Into thy arms for evermore, and thou shalt know these arms
So many times will they curl around thee
What we two knew before, how love and joy is the only good
In this world, then henceforth be loved, as only my heart can love
Stand up, look below; it is our lives at your feet
We step forth into the light of joy
The power of life we will enjoy, to satisfy our native wants
And I want thee!
For has it been not so from our very beginning
When this frail caravan called body, which is tenanted by soul
Fate takes the chart and with unfeeling fingers
Marks there one landmark, one pre-destined port of call
And although we hold the reigns of life
Fate gives us the chance to go by devious routes
Or travel in one direct line
Destiny ever stands by our sides
And though we may travel the whole world
In the end, we shall come to this one landmark.
As fate determined, it is destiny that drives life's caravan
So bring forth the silks and veils that did cover thy beauty
Careless and wild, ripe are thy lips, for the kiss of a lover
My lips shall feast upon thine, the lonely road, I no longer roam
We meet as one in our hearts' desire

Love, I speak to thy heart, thy heart that is always here
Oh! Draw thy lover deep to its sphere
Though thee and I are far apart, and yield by the spirit's art
Each distant gift that is dear,
Oh, my love, how I wish you were here.
Today our lips are far apart, yet draw thy lips to mine
Around and beneath and above
Is frost to bind and bar, but where I am, thee are
Desire and the fire thereof burns within me
Oh kiss me, kiss me, my love, thy heart is never far away
But ever with mine, forever without endeavour
Tomorrow love as yesterday when we did part
The hearts never astray, two souls, no power may sever
Together, my love, thy parted presence is ever with me

If I had words as golden as this birch has leaves
And if they took the light and shadow in their twist
Then I would let them dance about thy head
Delight thine eyes and caress thy face
Sifting and drifting to thy feet
Yet please accept these autumn leaves
They are more beautiful than all my words
I want for as long as it takes
The owls swoop down, the hawk falls
And the swallows swiftly curve
For thee to look towards me with love
I want to see when our lips touch
To always be the man in your arms
Is this too much to ask of life
The bright moment it takes a star to fall
I want thee for the first time to wake me
To find thee there softly shaking the curtain of thine hair
So that its heavy length falls darkly around my face
And I would have thee tie me closer
By its strands, the first time thee wake me

Sleep on, my love, in thy cold bed
Never to be disquieted
My last goodnight, thy will not wake
Till I thy fate shall overtake
Till age, of grief, or sickness must
Marry my body to that dust
It's so much love that fills this room
My heart keeps empty in my tomb
Stay for me there, I will not fail
To meet thee in this hollow vale
And think not much of my delay
I am already on the way
And follow thee with all speed
Desires can make, or sorrows breed
Each minute is a short degree
And every moment a step towards thee
'tis truth with shame and grief I yield
In thus adventuring to die
Before me, who more years might crave
A precedence in the grave

But hark, my pulse like a soft drum
Beats my approach, tells thee I come
And slow however my march may be
I shall at last sit down beside thee
The thought of this bids me to go on
And wait my dissolution
With hope and comfort, dear forgive
The crime, I love thee so
Divided but with half an heart
Till we shall meet and never part

Absence hear thou my protestation
Against thy strength, distance, and length
Do what thee can for alteration
For hearts of truest settle
Absence doth join, and time doth settle
Who loves a mistress of such quality
His mind hath found, affections ground
Beyond all time, place, and mortality
To hearts that cannot vary
Absence is present, time doth tarry
By thy absence, this good means I gain
That I can catch thee, where none may watch thee
In some close corner of my brain
There I embrace and kiss thee
And so enjoy, and none miss thee
Dearest Brenda, how I do love thee
As the birds do love the spring
As the bees their careful king
Then in requite, sweet Stott, Bush love me

Absent from thee, I languish still
They ask me not when I return
The straying fool will kill
To wish all day, all night to mourn
Dearest from thine arms let me fly
That my mind may prove
The torments it deserves to try
That tears my fixed heart from love
When weaned with a world of woe
To thy safe bosom I retire
Where love and peace and truth does flow
May I contented there expire
Lest, once more wandering from that heaven
I fall on some base heart unblest
Faithless to thee, false, unforgiving
May I lose my everlasting rest

My darling, I love thee as I love
Wild roses when first they bloom
With that soft miraculous blush of pink
As though some mischievous elf has painted them
Thee know the way they nod in the soft summer breeze
I never want to touch them, just stand and stare
That's how I love thee, dearest, the wild rose way
It is pure joy to look upon thy face
When I see wild roses, I see thee
Thee will always be you, never changing in my eyes
The same eternal summer
With the dew of life, ever sparkling in thine eyes
And ever fresh upon thy hair
May I never tire of thy touch
And the sweetness of those soft pink lips
Oh, how I hate this growing old that blinds
Our eyes and steals sweet laughter from our hearts
We should be together now
And stand still and stare at life's unutterable beauty

From dust I rise, and now, out of nothing, I awake
These bright regions which salute my eyes
Thy gift of love, with love I take
The earth, the seas, the light, the lofty skies
The sun and stars are mine, if thee I love
Then with hope, dearest, I am content to live
Forgive this crime, divided with but half a heart
Till on some shore, we shall meet and never part

By York Minster my love and I did meet
She walked o'er the Minster with her dainty feet
She bid me to take love easy, as leaves grow on the tree
But I, being foolish with her, would not agree
On the tower of York Minster my love and I did stand
And leaning on my shoulder, she laid her loving hand
She bid me to take life easy, as the moss grows on the portals
But I was foolish, and now full of tears

This love we have found
Is a beauty, is a joy forever
Its loveliness increases with time
It will never, never pass into nothingness
But always for ever and a day
Keep a quiet bower for us
And a sleep full of precious dreams
Therefore on every sorrow, we are
Wreathing a flowery band to bind us
Together with love and ecstasy

Naked thee lay clasped in my longing arms
I filled with love and thee with so many charms
To both equally inspired with eager fire
Melting through kindness, flaming in desire
With arms and legs, lips close in clinging embrace
Thee clutch me to thy breast
Thy nimble tongue, loves lesser lighting played
Within my mouth and to my thoughts conveyed
Swift orders that I should prepare to throw
Loves dissolving thunderbolt below
My fluttering soul, sprung with pointed kiss
Hang o'er thy beautiful brinks of bliss
Thy busy hand would guide that part,
That conveys my soul up to thy heart
And in moments of liquid rapture, I dissolve all
Melt into sperm, spent in every pore
One touch of thee was enough, smiling thee chide me
When with a thousand kisses, wandering over my panting bosom
Thee cry, all this to love's rapture due
Must we not pay a debt to pleasure too?
I am the most forlorn man alive
To show my wished obedience vainly strive
I sigh alas and kiss but cannot survive
Eager desires confound my first intent
Succeeding shame does more success prevent
And in frustration at last confirm me impotent
Even thy fair hand, which bids heat return to my frozen age
Applied to my dead cinder warms no more
Than fire to ashes could past flame restore
Trembling, confused, despairing
A wishing weak unmoved body I lie
This dart of love whose piercing point, oft tried
Which nature directed with such art

The ways are golden with leaves
That autumn blows about the air
The trees sing anthems of despair
And thee, my fair mistress, bind the locks of thine hair more loose
As thee weave more subtly thy spell over me.
Yes, children of love debonair
The laughter that lightly comes and reaves the garland from our sorrows' brow
Life rises up in full song
Joy fills our cup that flashes clear
The year fades in whispers now shadows and silence
Now winter is upon us two
As we lie beneath creamy clouds and a latticed sky
The hint of darkness, but decry a rosy flicker through the night
As we linger in the dusk

Novo Love
Death Of

Shaken, I know I'll wake this night after thee go,
Watching the soft shine on thy naked form,
Feeling thy buttocks, oh, my grief, thee take thy lover all in,
I think our love will not die, but there I go, trying to justify,
What are the chances of us two meeting in these circumstances again?
Thee may never know again the agony of pleasure thee brought me,
Fidelity is a dumb pain, God, yet I am lucky too!
The way they bring me through to ecstasy,
Despite my pride, ignorance, and exhaustion, yet thee were satisfied,
And so was I this night, thee never fail to show me,
A beautiful morning from every night,
And return me to living these my youngest years.

Silver Twist around Thy Wrist

Why do I place this around thy wrist, Brenda,
This silver twist, for what other reason,
But to show thee in part, thou my pretty captive art?
But thy bond-slave is my heart,
'tis but a silver thread that bindeth thee,
Snap the thread and thee are free,
But 'tis otherwise for me,
—I am bound and so fast bound,
So from thee I cannot go,
If I could, I would not so.

May I never above all forget my only love
To love thee, now when my thoughts hover over mountains
To the Midlands, resting their wings
Where fern-covered leaves hid our first meeting place
Cold is this earth
Seven wild Decembers from these woods have melted into spring
Faithful indeed is the spirit that remembers
Many years of pain and suffering
Thy noble heart, sweet love of youth forgive me
Whilst the world's tide bears me along
Sterner, darker hopes beset me
But cannot do thee wrong
No lighter light has brightened my heaven
No second morn has ever shone for me
From thy dear bliss my life is given
And all my life's bliss is with thee
Even when this golden day of dreams has perished
Despair was powerless to destroy
Then did I learn how love could be cherished
Strengthen and fed without the aid of joy
Then did I check the tears of useless passion
Weaned my soul from yearning after thee
Sternly denied its burning wish and even yet

I dare not languish, dare not indulge in memory's rapturous pain
Once drinking deep of thy love
How could I seek the world again
Come the wind may never blow again, as now it blows for us
The stars may never shine again as they shine
Long before October again returns
Seas of blood may crush the love in thy heart
And I this love is mine
No grief for grief can touch thee
If answering woe for woe
If any man can melt thee
Come to me now
I cannot be more lonely
My worn heart throbs wildly
'twill break for thee and when the world despises,
When heaven repels my prayers,
Will not thee comfort me?

Brenda, why should we delay,
Pleasures shorter than the day,
Could we, (which we never can),
Stretch our lives beyond their span?
Beauty like a shadow flies,
And our youth before us dies,
Or would youth and beauty stay,
Love hath wings, and will fly away,
Love hath swifter wings than time,
Change in love to heaven doth climb,
Gods, that never change their state,
Vary oft in love and hate,

Brenda, to this truth we owe,
All love betwixt us two,
Let not thee and I enquire,
What has been our past desire,
On what shepherds thee hath smiled,
On what nymphs I have beguiled,
Leave it to the planets too,
What hereafter we shalt do,
For the joys we now do prove,
Let us dwell on present love.

Brenda, let us live and love,
Let crabbed age talk what it will,
The sun goes down and returns above,
But we once dead, must be so still
Kiss me a thousand times, and then,
Give me one hundred kisses more,
And when this is done,
That our pleasures may remain,
We'll continue on our bliss,
By unkissing them all again.

Oh thou, my love, whose kiss upon my lips
Still seems my first thee whose summoning eyes
Even now the moment, show me each day love's world
A new sunrise each dawn, thy touch like a hand laid softly on my soul
Those tired brows of times
That mine oath has the keeping of,
What word can answer thy word?
What gaze to thine which now absorbs me within the sphere
Thy beautiful eyes hold me until I am mirrored
What embrace, thy kiss, my innermost heart does bound
Oh, lovely and beloved. Oh, my love!

Sunlit snows on sunlight dizzy craigs
Silvery streams in a haze of burnished gold
The fir-clad mountains bring peace untold
Here I sit in a pensive mood and callous nature
Upon thee, my love, to crown this morn
Far removed from the grime of towns
Let me sing to thee, my love, of this golden crown

Oh love, such happy days, such days as these
Must we waste them craving for the best
Like lovers o'er painted images of those, who,
Once their yearning hearts have blessed,
Have been happy on our day of rest?
Thine eyes say yes
But if it came again perchance, its ending would not seem so vain
O Love, turn from the unchanging sea and gaze down these steep slopes
Yet another year grown old
A dying mid-December's scented haze
That hangeth over Burntstump Hollow
Where the wind-bitten ancient elms enfold
Grey houses in half light
Long barns of love and red roofs stead
Wrought in days for men long since dead
Come down, oh love, may not our hands still meet
Since we live today
Forgetting not May deeming. August sweet
Oh, hearken, hearken, through that afternoon
The grey lovers sing a strange tinkling tune
Sweet, sweet, and sad
The toiling years, last breath too satiate of life to strive with death
And to us two will the New Year be not soft and kind?
That rest from life and pain from love which ne'er this end can gain
Darling of my heart, hear in this room
From love which ne'er this end can gain
Hark how the tune swells, that erstwhile did wain
Look up, love, ah cling close and never move
How can we have enough of life and love?
Of all the days that have passed o'er thine head
Shalt thee not wonder, looking from this bed
Through tree branches dark, on the windless east afire
That this day too thine heart doth still desire
Through changeless change of all seasons passing by

Do thee remember, my love, cowslips in a shady lane
Where we two walked sheltered by treed
On hanging spiders' webs thread the sun
Glides to and fro like who walks on a tight rope
And last the cuckoo mocks a mournful tune
Yet even trees lean back, whispering, 'I love thee'
And the shy blue, fly fussy bee
Yet all is so still, tick-tick I catch no not my heart
'tis my watch, then questioned by thee
I press a hand mockingly on my heart
Oh yes, thee my dearest heart, my joy, thee to as well
Lay closer to my thoughts than this shell
Then when shall we break for freedom soon enough?

The fountains mingle with the river
The rivers with the ocean
The winds of sweet heaven mix forever with fond emotion
Nothing in this world is single
All things by nature's law divine
In one another's being mingle
Why not my life with thine?
See the mountains kiss high heavens
And waves clasp one another
No sister flower would be forgiven
If it disdained its brother
The sunlight holds this earth
And moonbeams kiss the sea
Darling, what are all these kisses worth
If thou do not kiss me?
Yes, dawn will ache into another day
And leave us two naked
As yet we have to give and share, we have everything

Brenda's Asleep

Thy nerves tensed up and then
Thee have gone to sleep
Something not anchored in love drifts out of reach
Thee have gone to sleep, or feign sleep
It does not matter which
Into my head leaks bitterness
The throat dries up
The tongue swells up with complaints
Once sleep was simply sleep
The future stretched no further than
The pillows on which our heads rested
There were no awkward questions
No doubts caused love to fade
To a numbed kiss or trust to vanish
Thee have gone to sleep
A moment ago thy mouth upon mine
Thy sleep full of exhaustion, I cannot calm thee
There is no potion to wake thee
Do what I will say, what will I do
It is a sleep from which I am exiled

Slender, raven-coloured hair, joyful, young
Thee are kindred to lordly things
The wild ducks' flight, the white owls' wings
Pride of trees swiftness of streams
Magic of frost has shaped thy dreams
Thee have a kindly gracious power
The passion of the white syringa flower
Thee have a birthright no one can sell
And a secret joy no one can sell

From the desert I come to thee
And the winds are left behind
In the spread of my desire
Under thy window I stand
And midnight hears my cry
I love thee, I love thee with a love that shall not die
Till the sun grows cold
And the stars are old

Look from thy window and see my passion and pain
I lie upon the sands below and faint in disdain
Let the winds of the night touch thy brow
With the heat of my burning sighs
And melt thee to hear my vow
Of a love that shall never die
Until the leaves of the judgement book unfold

I would be pure, for there are those that care
I would be true, for there are those that trust me
I would be strong, for there is much to suffer
I would be brave, for there is much to dare
Are we not the weavers of our own dreams,
The makers of our own lives?
Are we not the love makers,
The movers and shakers of this world?
Then thee were gone

Still dwells thy beauty here
I listen in wonder at the sound of thy voice

Over the hills and dales, seemingly light years away
I turn my thoughts and remember this day
This when I first took thee for mine own
Beautiful, jaunty Brenda
Hath I not fallen in love with thee
I remember well thy hair, its raven hue
Thy lips as exciting, always fresh as the morning dew
Eyes a mystery never brown or yet hazel, always quite new
Yes, in that moment there was no other girl for me
In the wood hand in hand
We walked the twilight hours
Sharing moonlight, mist, and gentle showers
Just holding hands, two mortal lovers
Gentle, kind of wild nature was thee
Sweet lover perhaps it was all a dream to me

At length our sweet long kiss severed with such smart
As the last slow sudden drops were shed
From sparkling eyes, where all storm has fled
So singly flagged the pulses of each heart
Our bosoms shuddered with opening starts
Of married flowers to either side and spread
From knit stems, yet still our mouths burn red
Frowned on each other where apart we lay
Sleep sinks us lower than the tide of dreams
And as we watch our dreams sink away
Slowly our souls swim up again through gleams
Of watered light and dull drowned waifs of day
Till same wonder of new woods and streams
We awake and wondered more, and there we lay

Woodthorpe Park 1971
To think that I should walk around the park with thee,
And find eternity—and tomorrow too,
And dreams I thought had died or just were not true,
Walking with thy pale courage and the lemon essence of thy will,
That had been packed away a whole lifetime for some other day!
Was there traffic? Or did they stop, and what of other people? Did they stare?
I would have, if I'd been there watching us, walking around the park,
Without an earthly hope in view and yet thy arm across my shoulder,
Thy barest touch was such that my mind distracted for a moment,
From disastrous things found suddenly again that everything was there,
My friends steady and true, surety of purpose and of will and gentleness again,
Like water playing around a mill, still indefinite, like an echo from some
    far-off land
That in a childhood dream I knew, purity too crossed my mind,
Like a shaft of light that shines across a room when someone lifts the blind,
I found speech again and words that for a million years I had not dared utter,
Stumbled in certain force from out of me, shamelessly I clung to thee,
Oblivious for a moment, or was it two, until I realised in my dizzy mind,
Reeling with sky-high happiness that all we did was to walk around the park,
And say goodbye to all our yesterdays without each other, without love.

When do I see thee, most beloved one, in the light, the spirit of mine eyes,
Before they face their altar, solemnise,
The worship of that love through thee made known,
Or when in the dusk hours, we two alone, lay,
Close kissed and eloquent of still replies, the twilight,
Hidden glimmering visage lies, and my soul sees thy soul its own,
Oh! My Love, My Love, if no more should I see, nor on this earth,
The shadow of thyself, nor image of thine eyes in any spring,
How then should I sound upon life's darkening slopes,
The ground whirls and perishes, leaves of hope,
Then rush hour until we meet is as a bird that wings from,
His gradual way along the rustling of my soul,
His song still louder, trilled through leaves more deeply stirred,
Yet at the hour of our meeting, a clear word in every note he sings,
In love's own tongue yet, love though we knowest the sweet strain,
Suffers wrong, through our silent kisses, oft unheard.

In this fair stranger's eyes of brown
Thine eyes, my love, I see
I shiver, for the passing days
Hath borne me from thee

This curse of life, that not
A nobler, calmer train
Of wiser thoughts and feelings blot
Our passions from our brain

But each day brings petty dust
Our soon choked souls to fill
And we forget because we must
And not because we will

I struggle towards the light and thee
Whilst the night is chill
Upon times barren, stormy flow
Stay with me, Brenda, still

The mist that drifts away at dawn
Leaving but dew upon the grass
Which shall rise and gather into clouds
And not unlike the mist I have been
In the stillness of the night
I have walked with thee
And my spirit has entered your house
And your heartbeats were in my heart
Your breath upon my face, and I knew your all
Aye, I knew your joy, your pain

And in your sleep, your dreams were my dreams
I mirrored your summits, the bending of your slopes
Even the passing flocks of your thoughts and desires
And to my silence came laughter
But sweeter still than laughter, a greater longing came to me
It was boundless in thee
I beheld thee and loved thee
For what distances can love reach
What visions, what expectations can outsoar that flight
And like the seasons thee are also
Though in winter thee deny your spring
Yet spring reposing with you
Smiles in her drowsiness and is not offended
Thee have given to me my deeper thirsting after life
Surely there is no greater gift to man than this
And in this lies my honour
That whenever I come to thy fountain to drink
I find the living water thirsty
And it drinks me whilst I drink
For this I bless the most
Thee give much and know not what thee give at all
And if thee hear the whispering of my dreams
Thee will hear no other sound
Was it but yesterday we met in a dream?
True it is I have climbed hills and been in remote valleys
How could I have seen you?
Save from a great height or distance
How can one indeed be near unless he be far?
But in my solitude, I sought the secret of your joy and pain
And I, the believer, was also a doubter,
For often I have wounded myself that I might have
Greater love of thee and greater knowledge of you
Vague and nebulous is the beginning of all things, not their end
And I fain would have you remember me as a beginning
That which seems feeble and bewildering in us two
And in fact the strangest and most determined.

Is not our very breath that has affected and hardened our bones?
And is it not a dream that neither of us remember
Having dreamt that hast built lour love
Life and all love is conceived in the mist, not in a crystal
And who knows but a crystal is mist in decay
This I would have thee know in remembering
That which hast passed between us two
But thee do not see nor do thee hear.
The veil that clouds your eyes shall be lifted by my hands
And the clay that fills your ears shall be pierced
And thee will see and hear
But now our sleep has fled and our dreams are over
And dawn aches into naked day
And if in the twilight of memory we should meet once more
We shall embrace again, and thee will sing me a deeper song.

Joys are fleeting
But our love is anchored in the portals of dawn
Where heaven begins and heaven begins with us
God be with thee, dear heart
So dear to me
Too much for lovers' tongues to tell

Growing into the autumn of my years
Touched by thee in this wonder of love
Strongly aware of the joy and sorrow around me
Angry with this world which gives so much of its wealth
Angry with myself, for I know not what to do
I have become someone who drinks too much
As time flies by into pages of nothingness
Gently pushing fingers of memory into memories

Oh, fly away on silent wing
Ye gloomy owls of night
Look forward our two hearts from every hill
For every morning our love seems to say
There's something happy for us two on the way

Can thee touch thy lover now,
With thy soft beauteous lips
And increase thy love?
Can thee not touch me now with thy hand,
Directing me in thy path?
Now in thy stillness, pave the way for this love
Touch again the fondness of my fountain
And in my flow, say I love thee

I only know how true it is
That love is the chain of love
As nature is the chain of life
I keep my arms opened wide
I teeter on a tightrope stretched between
Thy need of me sometimes
By my need of thee
Balancing one foot before the other
Down the roads and rails of life
I kept my distance, trying hard
To keep the rules that bind us two
Yet there have been fences I have leapt
And some I have slid under
And all this goes with a wisp of smoke
When once more I am in your embrace

Oh dream, how sweet, too sweet, too bittersweet
Whose wakening should have been in paradise
Where souls brimful of love abide and meet
Where thirsting, longing eyes watch the slow door open
That opening, letting in, lets out no more
Yet and yet again come to me
That I might live again, my younger years

Come back again, that I might give
Pulse for pulse, breath for breath
Love for love, speak low, lean low
As but yesterday, my love
Yes, what are all these kisses worth,
If thou kiss not me?

Happiness Lane (Autumn)

The warm rain whispers, but the earth knows best,
And turns a deaf ear, waiting for the snow,
That white foam of bloom forgotten,
The rolling crest of green forgotten and the fruit swelling slow,
The shearing plough was here and cut the mould,
Shouldered over the sun-soaked land,
Letting the hot breath out for the quiet cold,
To reach down and comfort in its hands,
The sap ebbing from the tips of pine trees,
To the dry secret heart hiding away,
From the blade of grass still green with memories,
Down in the roots it closes the door of clay,
On this grief and growing and this late warm rain,
Babbling false promises in our Happiness Lane.

This is what I have chosen, this moment bitter and free,
From so much of thy life thee offered to me,
That gave life's most precious gift, love, a promised haven if need be,
But this is what I have chosen, this moment so bitter and free,
Come see what I have chosen in spite of thee,
Come look at the dust upon dead furniture that I see,
Come gape at this urban security that I have chosen,
From all that thee offered to me,
I have bought these bright tears with heartbreak,
And my useless tears, all jewels you'll see,
Adorning this moment I hast chosen, dark moments so bitter and free.

I will remember my oath to thee, I promise thee, whatever life may bring,
When river mists creep up the hill and chill and birds who love summer skies,
Tend their ways to kinder skies fearing that wild December,
I will remember, I promise thee, if ever life should bring some measure to our
Dearest dream and once again there should be spring and we two shall live
    to know
of all those dearest things, I promise thee,
Whatever may unfold, be there bitterness to reap, still in despair,
We'll never lightly hold this love we gave without a thought,
How could we this that was so dearly bought, and so, my love,
In spring, in summer, in autumn, and in December,
I will remember my oath to thee, I promise thee, whatever life may bring.

The Palace

Lying apart now, each in a separate bed,
He with a hook, keeping the light on late,
She like a girl, dreaming of her childhood,
All things elsewhere—it is as if they wait,
Some new event, the book he holds unread,
Her eyes fixed on the shadow overhead,
Tossed up like flotsam from a former passion,
How cool they lie, they hardly touch,
Or if they do, it is like a confession,
Of having little feeling—or too much,
Chastity faces them, a destination,
For which their whole lives were a preparation,
Strangely apart and yet strangely close together,
Silence between like a thread to hold,
And time and mind a feather,
Touching them briefly, do they not know they are old,
These two who are man and wife,
Whose fire hast now grown cold?

Thine is the form, the face heaven and earth hast turned to me,
And continuous beyond thy human features lie,
The mountain forms that rest against the skies,
With thine eyes, the reflecting rainbow, the sun's light,
Sees me all forests, flowers, birds and beasts,
Know this, my dearest one, and hold me forever in thy thought,
In creation's deep untroubled retrospect,
When thy hand touches mine, it is the earth's
That takes thy lover, deep grass, rocks and rivers,
Thy children still unborn, the love of ancestors,
Love, passed down from hand to hand,
Thy love, which comes from the creation of this world,
From those paternal fingers, streaming through clouds,
That break which light the colour of thy hair,
Here and now while I trace thy naked form with my fingers

Love's presence hast no end,
For these, thy arms that hold me, are the worlds,
In the two of us, the continents, clouds, and oceans meet,
Ourselves extensive with the night,
Lost! In our bodies worship, our hearts content do sleep.

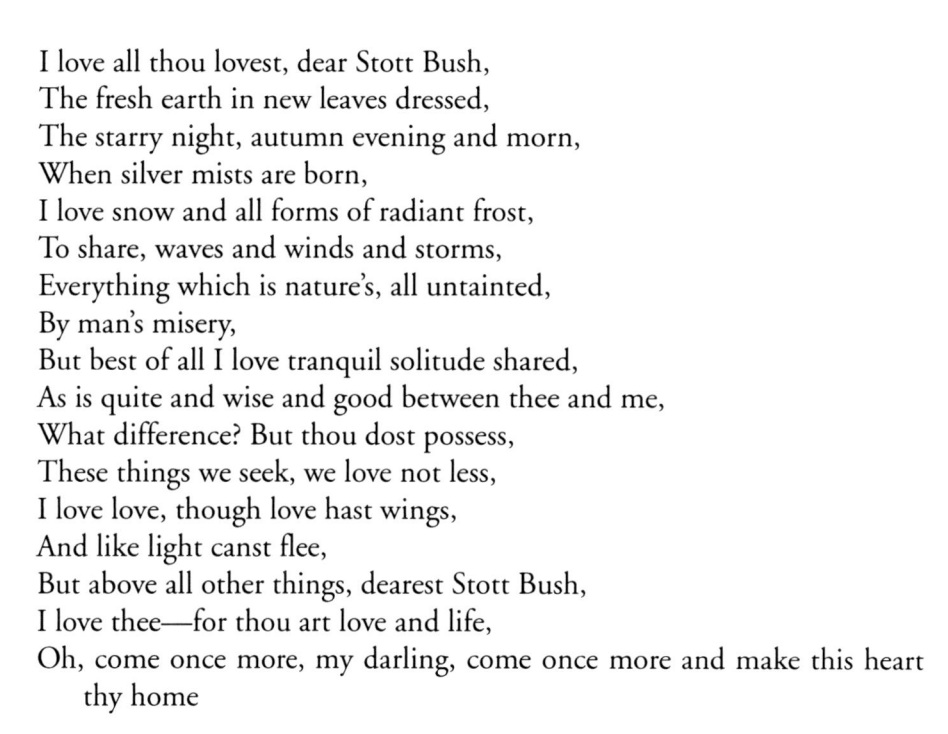

I love all thou lovest, dear Stott Bush,
The fresh earth in new leaves dressed,
The starry night, autumn evening and morn,
When silver mists are born,
I love snow and all forms of radiant frost,
To share, waves and winds and storms,
Everything which is nature's, all untainted,
By man's misery,
But best of all I love tranquil solitude shared,
As is quite and wise and good between thee and me,
What difference? But thou dost possess,
These things we seek, we love not less,
I love love, though love hast wings,
And like light canst flee,
But above all other things, dearest Stott Bush,
I love thee—for thou art love and life,
Oh, come once more, my darling, come once more and make this heart
    thy home

So many beautiful days, oh, so many days, seeing thee,
So tangible so close, how do I repay such joy, with what do I repay?
Now bloodthirsty spring has awakened in the woods,
The foxes start from their earths, and field mice drink the dew,
And I go with thee into the leaves, between the pines and silence,
Asking myself when will I be called to pay for the wonder of loving thee,
Of every thing I have ever seen, it is thee I want to go on seeing,
Of every thing I have touched, it is thee, thy flesh, I want to go on touching,
I love thy laughter; I am moved by the sight of thee sleeping,
What am I to do, love, my dearest loved one?
I do not know how others love, or how people have loved in the past,
I live, I move, I am thrilled watching thee, loving thee,
Being in love with thee is my very nature; thee please me more each time we meet,
Oh, where are thee I keep asking, if thine eyes should disappear,
How long is it since we last met, I think I am hurt,
I feel poor, foolish, and sad, for thee arrive and thee are lighting,
Glancing off the flowers that surround thee, that's why I love thee,
And yet I know not why there are so many reasons yet so few,
Has love always to be so involving, particular, and terrifying?
Honoured yet in mourning, flowering like the stars,
As soft as thy lips, and as measureless as thy kiss.

The Feather Hotel
November 1971

Here in the bedroom of this motel
We struggle for our holy ground
Our faces play discretion well
Our deepest anguish breaks no sound
The spirit's sole confession has
Swum in the crystal of one tear

We speak, and there is pain in words
And pain in heart that moves of them
We splinter mercy into shards
Yet stoop at once to gather them
A thousand deaths we take and give
A thousand deaths that we two may live

If one were evil, and one were true
We should not climb this long distress
I should destroy the truth in thee
Thee would corrupt my steadfastness
Yet here we wrestle right for right
As Jacob wrestled all a night

Nor thee nor I can ever gain
This last decision that we seek
Thy victory will be my pain
My triumph will be my defeat
We must now for this logic part
Twisting the wisdom of the heart

And yet this lens if spirit here
This crystal symbol in your eye
Denies the image of fear
Lend faith a new integrity
In this proud oracle we find
Love neither asks or grants an end

Then truths herself, the lie to fear
Blurs only edges of the mind
In the swift focus of a tear
Hesitancy of faith is found
Concreteness, now ebb the doubt

Now from thy soul my eyes remove
One after one each settled task
Intrusive fingers of thy love
Draw tendrils from my barren dusk

Truths inmost curtain opens wide
And there's no more place to hide

In loving thee only
Banner can we hoist
Is love itself
I take thy mound
With a white flag only
Thee may tear my life
But never my flag

What terrifies thy lover,
Is it the death of our love?
I see reflected in thy eyes
The surface of things
Thy heart takes
Loves rhythms are easily broken
To close for comfort, irregular leaps forward
Perhaps we are not prepared to meet
Pressures the conformity puts upon love
One way or another, I now see
How love varies, thee are still stronger than I
And apart from all else, have more experience
Of love's ways having loved others
Now in the tiny space between us
Thee stare, calmly at what I sense
With a thudding heart I realise thee have won,
And I have one more battle to come.

Speak my loved one's name softly
Let it linger in the air, let breeze carry it high
To the mountain tops, that snow in summer, to falling streams
That seek their meadowed fields, let the earth accept thy name
And make it part of all natural song, grasses that rustle as the wind steals by
Tell, oh, tell thy name, to every living inanimate thing
So as I wander by, I will not know whose sign whispers thy name
The earth or I that tell of the beauty of a soul that loved red earth
Oh, let not sorrow blind my eye, to beauty that thee can see
Let blessed birds fly, wheel, soar, and chatter to the eaves
Tell of thy name, all sounds of earth, that even when I sleep, my night
    thoughts, sing thy
name, Brenda, Brenda a . . .

When upon my bed reclining
Buried in the shadow of night
There hovers around me before mine eyes
Thy form of grace and light
As soon as quiet slumber
Hath closed my weary eyes
There softly thy image within my dreams arise
Oh, gather me unto thine arms
And press thy lips dear, close to mine
I want thee to make me warm
When I look into thy eyes
Cold want are soon forge d
All my earthly troubles fly
But with my dreams at morn
Thy image never fades
For within my heart thee dwell
Through all the life's long day

I see the flowers and spreading trees
I hear the wild birds singing
But what weary weight can please
And care my bosom wringing
Fain would I my grief impar t
Yet dare not for thy anger
This secret love will break my heart

I stand this night, where we two didst look out
Upon wooded hills and dales, where once lovers held hands
Before the winds how dark clouds flee
Lo! What a dreamer love hath made me!
A thousand fancies in this mood assail my restless mind
Mr spirit wills thee to my side, thy spirit appears
Thy whispers take thy lover in your arms
Kiss me and take this heart in thy keeping, my sweet dear
For where, ere I go I leave my heart behind my
But alas, where didst thou go?

It may happen that in some hidden middle night
Thee will rise up and come to me in solitude or silence
Yes, come to me in silence out of the noise of noon
Come, be the eye inside thy lover
Help me to drink up this river of thee
Stampede thee to bed and beyond, beyond
We will never meet in the same way as before
Come to me in solitude, pushing thy way through the crowd
There are no others here to pry and make demands
Yes, I will wait in solitude, that bring you here to me
I would only ask thee of this that thee ever be warm
Is this not the passport
The proven way for we two
To journey through a lifetime
Or just a single summer's day?

Our birth is but a sleep and forgetting
From dust arise, and from nothing now awake
The soul that arises within our life's star
Has had elsewhere the setting and cometh from afar
But in entire forgetfulness and not in utter nakedness
But trailing clouds of glory do we come
These brighter regions which salute my eyes
A gift of love, from thee I take
The earth, the seas, the light these loft skies
The sun and stars are mine, it's thee I prize
Never a stranger to my arms in this fair world
Yet strange and new to me, that thee should be mine
In love who nothing was that strangest of all
That brought you to me.

I am kissing thee
Even when I am not
I'm loving thee
Even when I m not
Hugging, embracing thee
Although thee are miles away
I am thinking how unfair this
That lies between us
A tear wells up and creeps
Down my cheek
Love is something
That thee cannot live or die without

Outside, the traffic drones, inside this room all is silent
A soft serenity rests now upon our hearts, as we lie hand in hand
In this deep peace that follows ecstasy—and this we know
Even while foolish tears, spring to our eyes as we go on alone
We hath known beauty which will last for all eternity
And love which men hath fought and died for, and not known
And so, my darling Stott Bush, free from bitterness
We gaze upon this room, another Eden we must leave
And sighing, we turn face to face, regretfully yet contented
A reluctant Adam and Eve

I love all thou lovest, dear Stott Bush,
The fresh earth in new leaves dressed,
The starry night, autumn evening and morn,
When silver mists are born,
I love snow and all forms of radiant frost,
To share, waves and winds and storms,
Everything which is natures, all untainted,
By man's misery,
But best of all, I love tranquil solitude shared,
As is quite and wise and good between thee and me,
What difference? But thou dost possess,
These things we seek, we love not less,
I love love, though love hast wings,
And like light canst flee,
But above all other things, dearest Stott Bush,
I love thee—for thou art love and life,
Oh, come once more, my darling, come once more and make this heart thy.

There is a name,
For whose soft sound would not I abandon all,
This conformity, this pomp would have had thee call,
Some sweet title of beloved shame,
Gold coronets be seemly, but bright flame,
I choose thee, my gal; for thee I would let fall,
All crowns, all kingdoms, all flesh,
Just for one caress of thine, one kiss my soul to tame,
I crown thee my queen, but sooner call thee lover!
I bid thee hasten, nay, I plead thee,
Come in the shadow of night to my bed,
Heed not my sighs, but eagerly uncover,
As mouths mingle, my sweet soft infamy,
And rob thy lover of his maidenhead, (spring),
Lie close, no pity, but endless love,
Kiss me but once and my pain is paid,
Hurt me or soothe me, stretch out one limb above,
Like a strong man who would constrain a maid,
Touch me, I tremble, and my lips turn back,
My mouth finds thy mouth, is there ought we lack?
To thy desire, till love is one with us two.
Brenda! I shall faint with ecstasy, I hide my face,
For shame at my passion, I am disturbed, I cannot rise,
I breathe hard with thy breath, thy exquisite embrace,
Crushes, thy teeth are agony, pain dies,
In deadly passion. Ah! Brenda thee come—thee thrill thy lover,
Bite, bite for Christ's sake, bite,
Ah! Love's fountain spreads o'er me.

Of woman's delight and man's desire, in this there is no weariness,
To feel the fury of the fire and writhe in thy close caress,
Of thy fierce embrace and wanton kiss, and final nuptial night,
How sweet a passion, shame, is this. Ah Brenda, thy love is my delight,
Free men can cast an eye on thy sweet charms and seek by word and touch,
With thee to lie, and vainly to feel thy buttocks on the sly,
Ah! God of love, grant me one more night, to this our sweet mystery,
To feel thee move beneath me, laid prone upon the couch of lust and shame,
To feel thee rise my hot blood within like a virgin maid,
And my great sword of passion within thee flame, to kiss and clasp thee tight,
This is my joy without a name, oh Brenda, thy love is my delight,
To feel again my love grow grand, touched by the languor of thy kiss,
To lie between thy thighs and feel thee suck the hot blood from my gland,
Mingled with fierce spunk that does hiss and boil in sudden spurted bliss,
Oh love, the long-drawn-out fight, grant me eternity of this!
And stay with me once more beyond the dawn of light,
Ah Brenda, my love thee are my only delight.

Thee cannot alter what my heart is saying
Thee cannot change its song
Transpose a key to be more kind
My heart will know you're wrong
But do not falter from this game we are playing
Like foolish things it's brief
But in its foolishness I find
My heart's a secret place
I lay in your arms close to your heart
We were the ends of the world apart
Our hands did not touch to say goodbye
And we were as near as tears as to a sigh
Eternity is life when love has gone
There is no sunset, and no dawn
Only the dead monotonous grey
Of some interminable day

Happiness is something
That does not come at will
It comes with helping others
With joy their hearts to fill
It comes in the most simplest way
So spread a kindly smile along life's way
For everyone that you pass on
Also makes your life worthwhile
Those who now sow courtesy reap friendship
Those who sow kindness gather love
Having no one to share your joy
Is as bad as having no one to share your sorrows

The summer has crossed the sky now
And is slowly sinking a perfect orange circle
It seems heavy a grief-laden tear
Too quelled with sorrow to keep back any longer
Rolling down the face of day
Soon to fall into the darkness of night

Draw thy mantle close around thee
Amidst the fading echo of summer
And walk slowly with thy lover
Smell the coming autumn in the trees
Watch the bonfire smoke twist and swirl
See the last leaves fall
And darling, think of me

Thine am I, my faithful love
Thine, my lovely Brenda
Every pulse along my veins
Every roving fancy
To thy bosom I lay my heart
There to throb and languish
The despair has rung its core
That it would heal its anguish
Take away thy rosy lips
Rich with balmy treasure
Turn away thine eyes of love
Lest I should die of pleasure
What is life when wanting love,
A night without morning?
Love's the cloudless summer sun
Nature's gay adorning

Whatever thee wish to do or dream
Thee must begin it now, for tomorrow is too late
Boldness has a genius, power, and magic of its own
Begin to live and love, now, my love
For life's joys are many
Especially those given in love

The evil of the world sinks away
My own sins and troubles fall away
As we watch shadows lengthen as our day draws nigh
Oh, my love, your lover sighs
Thy love is held externally
On this soft summer air
Our going of separate ways
Brings sadness to this heart

Our bodies stretched bathing in the sun
Through this deep June day
The leaves of all colours of green and gold
They spin through the Trent Valley as the winds blow
The float mirrored in the forest and blue sky
The short hours of our love go by
I think of thee who hast loved me these many years

Clouds hold her, cirrus and stratus fold thee
Cumulus wrap round thee, hill mists and sea
Shrouds the ground, sun take and wind's life three
Light fill thy life
Memories stay with me

Through all abstract reasoning
Driving down the M1 flat out, deserted of cars
Drowsy with sleep, half a bottle of brandy gone
Then in a moment, I jerk alive
Something passed through my being
That alters and enlightens
This I feel, realisation of what has passed
Between us two was real
My nerve ends tingle; uncoded messages
Whisper up and down my spine
I care for thee, for love of thee I cared

Something has passed a finger through all abstract reasoning
From love I sheltered, outside of love
But still the humanity, emotion leaked in
Unprepared, struck, stunned so suddenly by thy identity
How can I hold on to any revelations?
Thee have moved so quietly into my life

Thy kiss humid, soft seal of affection
Tendered pledge of future bliss
Speaking, silence, a dumb confession
Passions birth and lovers play, chaste concession
Glowing dawn of this bright day
Surrendering joy, adieus' last action
When lingering lips no more must join
What words of mine can speak affection
As thrilling and passionate as thine
What is this strange feeling at the time of parting?
Is it that I do not give enough of myself to thee?

April cannot make up her mind
First she laughs and then she cries
Now she's sulky, now she's kind
One moment weeping, next blue skies
Confused she smiles summer smiles
Then turns towards winter and cools
Her moods last such a little while
She makes us all her April Fool

Stott Bush, how often I dream of thee
After these years and years
Then again we are in harmony
I am again on the edge of thy mystery
Thee again on the edge of me, awake then
I know that thee need me
But then, oh then, I know that I love thee
129 miles always, two hours ten minutes in time
It is so frustrating. When will I see thee?

Learn to look beyond the mask of life's unsmiling face
Beauty can be found in the features of life's most common place
Let us seek whatever things are good and true
In other words, let we two make our own magic
Let us also be content with this power love hast given us two

So beautiful this early morn
Driving into the dawn
Watching with awe the darkness of night
The black clouds flee before my eyes
And as the golden head of the sun appears
Over the low hills of Salisbury Plain on a brand-new day
Despairs of night are forgotten and my heart sings
How I wish thee were by my side to share this joy!

All that I thought too sweet to have
All that I most desire
As one that in dim water dips his hands
So that I would feel the strands
Of thy hair rippling through my hands
And cool forever the fever of thy lips
Cease all care and strife
An interchange of song and sin
Thy hide my hands, my lips within
The sweet oblivion of thy hair

Love can only be reached through love
Faith by sharing faith
Courage by reaching out thy hand to courage
If we two share these things,
Then through the love we share,
We will share the impossible
And endure all adversity

Thy beauty and love are all but a dream
They change not with the changing day
Thy love stays forever like a stream
That flows but never flows away
Thy beauty as bright as the sun's bow
That blossoms on the spray of flowers
Thy calm, proud body, thy walk of angels
Take of me what is not my own, my love
The pain is mine alone

Parting is such sweet sorrow
I pray that thee have a safe journey
So we must say goodbye, my darling
And go, as lovers go, forever
Tonight remains to pack, and fix labels
And make an end of lying down together
I watch thee slip thy dress below thy knees
I lie so still; I hear the rustling of your comb
So many countless things I remember
Thee are now gone from me, all that remains
A cup half empty, lipstick stains a paper tissue
As I gaze into the silence of the night
My thoughts wander, wander to distant lands
Thee are so near yet so far
A lingering scent of love that never dies
I think of thee. I love the one who cares for me
We a moment ago were alone so in love
Like a penetrating storm it lingers on
Setting the pace for our world

Where the load water fall below
Making wind among the flowers
Love, the love springtime comes and goes
Yet we know the summer awaits our souls

I am fire stilled by water
A wave, lifting from the abyss
In my veins, the moon-drawn tide arises
Into a tree of flowers scattered in sea foam
I am air caught in a net
The prophetic bird that sings in the sky
I am a dream before nothingness
I am a crown of stars
I am the way of love
Oh, thou art my life, my way
If passion bid me flee, my reason shall obey
No further from me to thee
Mistress mine, thou art the light in me

Thine hand trembles against mine
I want to breathe for nothing else but thy possession
Now, flow this evening before the dawn
Shakes its bright sun in the sky
Thee let me lie one night in thine arms
And give unto thy lover peace
Stand by me, love, lest the dark day
Should hurt me more than I should know
I beg that if the wound grows sharp
Thee take me when I ask to go
Step closer love and dry those brown eyes
What's marred you will never mend by tears
Let's finish where thee tale began
And kiss away the ruined years

A sudden mild day in November
When it seems the year had no more to say
At autumn's whisper, the summer turned away
Now when all is grey, thy fragrance is everywhere
Winds have blown since thee were in my arms
And then hurried away from me
Now a breeze recalls thee

Far in my mind, of all mankind
I love but thee alone
For I will prove that faithful love
Is devoid of shame
In thy distress and heaviness
To part with the same
And sure all, though that do not so
True lovers are they none
For so that I thy company have
I ask no more
From which to part it maketh my heart
As cold as any stone
I have been part of thy joy and bliss
I must also part of thy woe endure
But now adieu, the day cometh fast
For in my mind and that of all mankind
I love but thee alone

The day is done, and darkness falls
In one step from the wings of night
As a feather is wafted downwards
From a hawk in his flight
To see again thy face gleam through this fading light
And a feeling of sadness and longing
That akin to pain
Comes o'er me; come, my love, read me some poem
And this night shall be
Filled with music and the cares
That infest the day
Shall fold their tents
Like the Arabs and silently seal away

There is no bridge that love cannot cross
There is no world that love cannot live
Love is more peaceful than death
Does not our life lead into another?
When thee go down that long road of life
Thee will meet thy love again
And again possess all that thee hast lost
Sleep but to awaken to a new life
Like a long breath all these years

When love with unconfined wings
Hover within my soul
And all my divine Brenda brings
A whisper within my thoughts
When I lie tangled in thy hair
And fettered to thy brown eyes
The birds of the air, knew not such liberty
When flowering cups run swiftly
With alloying Thames
Our careless heads with roses crowned
Our hearts with loyal flames
When thirsty grief in wine me sleep
If we have freedom in our love
When health and droughts go free
Angels alone that soar above
Enjoy no such liberty

I wish nothing now
Except to stay here in your arms
Spent! Even as this day
These arms to road's end
And you are tired, tired face
Already reaching into sleep
The climax of the day

But in this Indian summer we have known
A sunset blaze before we part
Our love's like an autumn rose
Which opens wide to show its tender heart
Heavy with fragrance as petals fall
Sweetest is all my love, sweetest of all

Wherever I may be, in the woods or in the fields
Whatever the hour of day, be it dawn or in the eventide
My heart still feels it yet
This eternal regret
As I sink into my fitful sleep
Thee my absent one is near
Alone on my couch
I feel thy loving touch, and it is whether in repose or in work
We are forever close

Thee have gone into the world of light
And I alone sit lingering here
Thy face is fair and bright, and my sad thoughts do clear
Thy love glows and warms my breast, like stars upon some gloomy grove
Of these faint beams in which this hill is dressed after sun's remove
I see thee walking in the air if glory
Whose light does trample on all my joys
My days which at best, but dull and hoary
Meet glimmerings and decays
Oh, holy hope, and high humidity, high as the heavens above
These are thy walks, and thee have shown them to me
To kindle my cold love

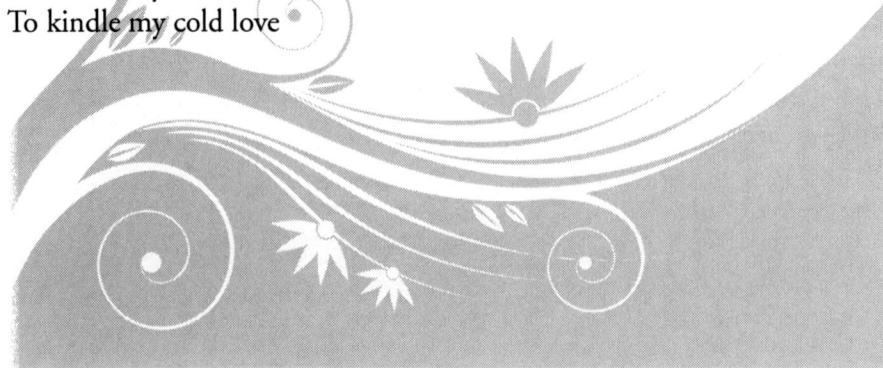

My Love

Upon a gloomy night, with all my cares to loving flushed,
Oh, venture of delight, with no one in sight,
In safety, in darkness up the stair I crept
O, happy enterprise, concealed from others' eyes,
When all the world in silence slept, upon a beauteous night.

I went without discerning and with no other light,
Except that for which my heart was burning, it lit and led me through,
More certain than the light of noonday clear,
To thee who waited near, whose presence I knew well,
Oh night, that was my guide, oh darkness, dearer than the morning's pride.

Oh night, that joined the lovers, transfiguring them each into the other,
'tis that within my throbbing breast, which only for thee entire I save,
Over ramparts fanned fresh wind fluttered, lulled by airs which cedars wave,
To my rest I sank, and all thy gifts thee gave,
Until every sense suspended by thy caresses and all my cares releasing,
Thy neck I wounded unthinking, so rapt was I, so swept away.

Lost to myself I stayed, my face upon my lover laid,
From all endeavour ceasing, and from all my cares releasing,
This sudden sense of out flowing, my soul I felt revealing,
The man who truly there has come,
This gift that leaves men knowing naught, yet passing knowledge with their thought.

Well dost thou, love thy Solomon Feast to hold in vestal February
Not rather choosing out some rosy day
From the rich coronet of the coming May
When all things meet to marry
O quick, procvernal power
That signalled punctual through sleepy mould
The snowdrops time to flower
Fair as the rash oath of virginity
Which is first—love's first cry
Of baby spring
That fluttering sudden beneath the breast of earth
A month before the birth
Whence the peaceful poignancy
The joy contents
Sadder than sorrow, sweeter than delight
That bequeaths now the breath of everything
Though each one sighs as if to each alone
The cherished pang was known
At dusk of dawn, on his dark spray apart
With it the blackbird breaks the young day's heart
In evenings hush
About it talks the heavenly minded thrush
Of the hill with like remorse

Smile to the sun's smile in his westering course
The fishes drooping skiff
In yonder bay sheltering
The clouds that call upon the shining cliffs
The children noisy in the setting ray
Own the sweet season, each thing as it may
Thoughts of strange kindness and forgotten peace
In me increase and tears arise
Within my happy, happy, mistresses eyes
And lo, her lips averted from my kiss
Ask from lovers' bounty, much more than bliss
Is not the sequestered and exceeding sweet of dear desire
Electing his defeat?

When thee and I go down, breathless cold,
Our faces both worn back, to earthly mould,
How lonely both shall be, I without thee, thee without me?
I cannot bear the thought, thee may first die,
Nor of how thee would weep, should I,
We two are too much apart, what can we do.
To make our bodies one—thee I, me thee,
We are most nearly born, one of the same kind,
We have the same delight, the same true mind,
Must we then part, is there no other way,
To keep a beating heart and light of day?
I could now rise and run to meet thee,
To where thy are breathing—you
That we might meet and thy living voice,
Might sound above all fear and we two rejoice, within our love.
How frail the body is, and we are made,
As only in decay to lean and fade,
We think too much of death, there is gloom,
When I cannot hear thy voice in some room.
O, but how suddenly, either may droop,
Then there may be a place where fading flowers,
Drop—lifeless face, through weeping hours, is there nothing safe?
Can we not find some everlasting life, in our one mind?
To understand thy spirit through thy word, or by thy hand,
We can find a way through love, can we not reach beyond, body, flesh?
When thee or I must go down evermore, there'll be no more to say,
I love thee, I do, I do, I do, I do, I do.
Oh, my true love, for I'll not be sad, for love left unsaid.

To Spring

This naked earth is warm with spring,
and with green grass and bursting trees,
Leans to the sun's glorying gaze,
Life is all colour and warmth and light,
Striving evermore for these,
He is dead who cannot see or feel,
Or take the warmth and life from the glowing earth,
And when this burning moment breaks,
All other things are out of mind,
The day shall take thee and clasp thee with strong arms,
And night enfold thee with soft wings.

What adventure of the spirit, new goal set and new crown given?
What new earth, new sea, new heaven, for life's love to inherit,
Horizons where the sea and sky meet and merge in ecstasy:
Horizons where great tides run, blood tinctured by the setting sun,
Where the soul is caught beyond all sense, beyond all thought,
This that makes us one with the first force of things,
Past even love's imaginings, past all earthly wings.
We two have felt this, heard where we listened, by the wood along the lane,
Where the spangled raindrops glistened upon leaves and grasses at our feet,
and rain—pearls palely glowed upon bare boughs, like an infant newly
    christened
Hark do thee not hear even now the sharp insistent beat of raindrops,
Where we tasted love, how sweet?
Listening, we heard until the last throb, down the deserts of the wind:
A silence, that fell, save for the rush of windy voices saying hush,
And in that silence did we not hear well the beating of our hearts upon
the wind, faint, tumultuous and remote, What strange bridal, kisses sublime,
Soul and body hath no bonds to lovers as they lay upon, stay with me here,
Yet now thee must be leaving. Oh no! I promise to love thee, dearest,
What adventure of the spirit, what sorrow in parting!

Come to me in the silence of night
Come in the speaking silence of a dream
Thy soft rounded cheeks and eyes so brown
As bright as the sunlight on a mountain stream
Yes, always, come back even in tears
Thee whom I hast loved for years
Thou, my love, my only love
Whose kiss upon my lips still seems the first
Whose summoning eyes, even now
As our love-world, new sunrise, shed every dawn
Whose voice, attuned above
All modulation of the deep-bowered dove
Is like a hand softly laid upon my soul
What embrace, what kiss mine innermost heart can't prove
For one who sees the great sun freeze
As he wonders from hill to hill
All thy heart dearest is a woven part
Of the flurry and drift of snow-white clouds
I feel the stir of the years
As they go past us two, upon the wind
By night by day, we heed no thing
Or the needs of spring, of autumn's wonder
Or winters chill love so long ago

If love is not worth loving
Then life is not worth living
Nor ought is worth remembering, but well forgot
For store is not worth storing
And gifts ate not worth giving
If love is not
And idly cold is death cold
And life heat idly hot
And vain is any offering
And vainer still is any receiving
And vanities of vanities is our lot
Better that life's heaving heart is death's unheaving
Better than the opening leaves, than leaves that rot
For there is nothing left worth achieving or receiving
If love is not

Come to me in the silence of the night
Come to me in the speaking silence of a dream
Come with soft round cheeks, and eyes so bright
As in the sunlight of a stream
Come back in tears
O Brenda, my hope, my love of these past years
Oh dream, how sweet, too sweet, too bittersweet
Whose wakening should have been in paradise
Where souls brim full of love, abide and meet
Where thirsting, longing eyes

Watch the slow door that opens
Letting in, lets no more out
Yes, come to me in dreams
That I may live my life again
Come back to me in dreams, that I may give
Pulse for pulse, breath for breath
Kiss for kiss, speak low
As long ago, my love, how long

He climbed Ben Nevis and looked northwards
To the land of his father's birth
He beheld Scotland through the mist
Then the gates of his heart were flung open
And his joy flew far over this land
He closed his eyes, and in the silence of his soul
A sadness came upon him
As he descended the mountain, he thought in his heart
How shall I go in peace, without sorrow?
Not without a wound in the spirit shall I leave this mountain
Long were the hours of pain and loneliness upon the slopes
And who can depart from his pain and aloneness
Without regret to many fragments of the spirit
Have I scattered here
Too many children of my longing walk naked among these hills
I cannot withdraw from them without a burden and ache within my soul
For it is not a garment I cast off this day
But my skin I tear off, with my own hands
Nor is it my thoughts I leave behind me
But a heart made sweet with hunger and thirst
Yet I cannot tarry longer
The mountain that calls me, calls all things unto love
Fain would I take all things that are here
But how shall I?

Do you remember those days gone by?
Far from the maddening crowd amongst the trees
Where all we wished to do was lie
Lulled by the soft and scented breezes
Of summer days in the wood
When all nature was in the mood
That thrilling touch upon thy thigh
As hands crept over stocking tops
Of sensations rising high
I will die of course if thee do not love me
But it will be a quick clean death
It will be all the stab of springtime joy and love
When it was young knowing no defect
No thought of shame
No need to phrase-rephrase a sing thing
No need for the lowering of eyelids
No need for undecided pauses pointing up desire
No need to cloak oneself in lies
For it will be death I know
But not a sickly one or of moribund excuses
It will be sharp and quick like ice cold water
It will be steel
It will sting
It will be the last sharp intake of breath
The day thee tell me no!
I have no desire for my Jonathan
I'll die a pure and instantaneous death
So come with me and be my love
We two will great displeasure show
For all the littleness of life
We will live within a moment's pause
Transfixed with each other's sighs
Just browse about each other's minds
Till death itself passes us by
Let us seek oblivion under a blue sky
Where placid sea meets placid sky
I'll climb some lonely mountain crest
Just to catch thine eye

When the day unrolls itself from second sleep
Reluctantly I awake, shower, choose a tie
These daily things are cheap
The small wage to keep my nightmares small
Trivial, dull, not terrible at all

Draw nigh, sweet love, violets at birth
Pale lilies tinged with crimson, as snow
At dawn approach, the pansy, darksome dye
Deepens when tender winds blow o'er it
And gives its beauty to the summer gaze
So, dearest love, blush at being mine, yet gently come
And place thine hand within mine
Thine too delicate to crush into warmth
Save that blood mantling to thy cheek shall flow
And so I will not hesitate to put
A ring upon thy hand, my sweet mystery
O love's devices, to a shadow in our hearts
This eternity of an immortal self
That is, and shall be while stars endure
Or while the god of love is pitiful, of all men's sorrows
Ah, joys are fleeting
But our love is anchored in the portals of dawn
Where heaven begins and heaven begins with us
Oh heart, so dear to me
So much beloved for lover's tongue to tell

In the mirror of my mind there has always been thee
A reflection of a heart that can be naught but true
Thy eyes, thy smile, your exquisite style
Just the tenderness of thy touch
Never ceases to move this guy so much
There's ever more than there's to behold
Such bliss, happiness, and joy untold

All beauties in fact all thee coming after, can but shed their splendour
And heave a sigh of despair, for thee, my love, are beyond compare
Cast on us two an eternal spell, I vow to love thee and keep thee well
Onward then with our love, with thee, my love
This land we will walk hand in hand
Until journey's end, I know not what lies beyond
Be it nothingness or a new dawn, but with thee, my love
I shall rejoice, for my choice is thee, my love

This everything now, the quick delusion of flowers
The colours of this bright summer's wood
And the soft blue spread of heaven, the bees' song
Is this everything, we two desire, a dream
The unconscious cry of power for deliverance
The distant line of hills, that beautifully rest in blue
Only the wild strain of fermenting nature
Only grief, only agony meaninglessly, fumbling
Never resting, yet never a movement
No! Leave us two alone thy impure dream, of a suffering world
A breath of wind cools our cheeks, it is time to go
We walk together through the quiet beauty of the afternoon
Alone but not lonely, winds are singing in the pines
And birds chanting softly through the still air
I felt thy love, the friendliness of trees clad in shining green grass
The pure scent of bluebells and pine
Borne on the gentle air that kissed us two as we passed
And that was all, yet in these simple things, our hearts found peace
Is this not true of us two, the beauty of the ages lie for all who seek

As dawn comes gently o'er the land
Stay from mine eyes that I may sleep
Nor wake the sadness of my thoughts again
My pains are stilled in sleep—I do not weep
I dream of health and pain-free days
Days that have passed with fading youth
So, sleep, stay within my eyes, oh world, recede from me
I cannot face the truth.
It will not come again, yesterday's love

Quietly before the birds awake
Suddenly in the predawn of time
My life is no longer my own
Self-pity and despair have gone, I am for thee
Quietly closing doors so not to wake my life before
With my heart as light as the morning mist
I come to thee, to our rendezvous
When thy warm hands reach out for mine
And thee whisper 'kiss me'
The love in my heart for thee is too much to bear
So here I am to caress the future not the past
Love for each other will last beyond time

I must not think of thee tired yet strong
I shun all thoughts of daylight that lurks
The thought of thee, and in my arms heaven's delight
And in the dearest passage of song
Oh, just beyond the sweetest though that throng
This breast, the thought of thee, waits hidden yet bright
But it must never, never come in sight
I must stop short of thee, the whole day long
But when sleep comes to close each difficult day
When night gives pause, to the long watch I keep
And all my bonds depart, must doff my will
As raiment laid away
With first dream that comes with first sleep
I run, I run forever am I captured in thine arms

The warm rain whispers, but the earth knows best
And turns a deaf ear, waiting for the snow
That white foam of bloom forgotten
The rolling crest of green forgotten, and the fruit swelling slow
The shearing plough was here and cut the mold
Shouldered over the sun-soaked land
Letting the hot breath out for the quiet cold

To reach down and comfort in its hands
The sap ebbing from the tips of pine trees
To the dry secret heart hiding away
From the blade of grass still green with memories
Down in the roots it closes the door of clay
On this grief and growing and this late warm rain
Babbling false promises in our Happiness Lane

Incautiously, unheeding, thinking themselves alone
The lovers walk, firm in their belief
Under the pine fringes of the wood
Oblivious to the changes of the season
The cones and needles worn
The end of summer hidden in the sap
Unperceiving and inhuman, we trained not to see
Now see, from the moment's happenings
The startled flash of time
The bough breaking underfoot
To the sameness of infinity
The oblivion of love and hope
Hoping that they will not turn and cast
One last and sudden disillusioned glance
At the memories of love
To see the trackers and thieves of happiness
sodden in the underbrush

All thoughts, all passions, all delights, whatever stirs my mortal frame
All are but ministers of love and feed my sacred flame
Often in my waking dreams, do I live o'er again my happy hours
When we together hath lain, in many wooded towers
With moonshine often stealing o'er the scene, had blended with the light dusk
And thee were there, my hope, my joy, my own dearest Brenda
Thee leant against my side and listened in lingering light
For sorrows hath we known as well as joy, hope, my love
Thee who knows me best and hast truly loved me where birds do sing

I reside within myself and let this day grow dark
I lie awake all night, sighing till daylight
No matter how much I mourn
Will I ever see thee again?
Thy spirit on the mountainside
Under the wings of eagles
I struggle over ridges and climb the summit
Searching all the time, I see thee not

After the drums of time have rolled and ceased
Shall life renew truth our love
Or death will he annul, all tears assuage
Or fill these void veins full again with youth
And wash, with immortal water, age
When I do ask thee, Brenda, thee say not so
My head hangs weighed with sorrow
And when I hearken to the earth, she says
My fiery heart shrinks, aching, it is dead
My ancient scars shall not be glorified
Nor my silent tears within be dried

I'll never pursue the wandering dove
But still the charm in thee I approve
Though I deplore the change in thee
In hours of bliss we oft have met
They could not always last
And though the present I regret
I'm still in love with the past
I know her number off by heart
It has a magic spell
And as my fingers start to dial
My heart starts to pound
Two six nought one seven one
Silence—click-click
Then burr, burr, contact is sought
It's ringing, yes, yes
But it is unsatisfactory
Echos—less nothing—unanswering way
The burring goes on burring
My pounding turns to pain
My whole reason for living
Seems to ebb away in vain
No one to share my loneliness
Or to feel my despair
As the phone goes on ringing
And I know my love is not there

Slender, joyful, young, raven-coloured hair
For thee are kindred to lordly things
The wild geese flight, the white owl's wings
Pride of trees, swiftness of gliding streams
Magic of frost upon a winter's morn
These things have shaped thy dreams
Thee have a secret birthright no man may sell
A secret joy of only thee can tell

Climbing alone all day, in this blazing waste of snow
I move down with the sunset's edge, to the highest meadow
Into the cold mists of spidery waterfalls, to the cobweb of water
Woven with incredible bright flower of Iris
And now rising between high mountains, a human form
As I stood entranced amidst the whirling water
I was caught in a vision of thee
More real than reality, fire shone in the deepest curves of thy bosom
Thy cheeks were snow flushed
Thy tender arms seemed to be swimming through lead
Making a fluorescent cobweb of light though the trees
Thy thighs exact curves, slipping through my hands
And thee tense, upon the verge of abandon
The sweet odour of thy sex, thee in all thy splendid nakedness
The wind blowing in thy raven tangled hair
Burning passionate, against impassive snow-covered peaks
This moment of fact and vision, seizes immortality
Thee become the person of this place
Thine the responsibility of love realised and beauty
Real beyond flower or stone
Yet in this world is there no way
The stage cries even on the remotest mountain
Thee vanish from mine eyes, and I am alone

Be a goddess and hold me with thy charms
Be a woman and hold me with thine arms
Teach me, only teach me to love as I ought
I will speak thy speech of love, think thy thought
Meet if thou require it, both demands
Laying both flesh and spirit in thine hands
Thou shall be tomorrow, not tonight
I must always bury tomorrow out of sight
Must weep a little love, foolish me
And so to fall asleep, love, loved by thee
But as I drift into sleep, I hear thee say
Those tired sweet drowsy words we left unsaid
Sleep well, love, for I follow thee
Till time blurs our distance between, where thee roam
And with wild songs of evilness
Recall thee to these arms
That was for a short while thy home

When autumn sun glows upon the flowers
Or ripples down the dancing sea
Thy, with thy passionate powers
Beleaguered and bewildered me
Within the autumn woods
Within the breath of winter's silence
The spirit stirs and broods

As soon as evening wandered down the air
We sat bewitched, and drank nectar rare
Of the dew, sunset and scattered flowers
Till lastly rose the moon
And came the enchanted hours
Thoughts that shun the day, bedeviling
Nightmares, fantasies on timid wings
Think on these things
I, but for thee, in slumber would have lain
Missing these lovely things

When I think of all the happy hours
I have spent with thee, my only love
And know the miles that now lay between us two
How can I but be sad
How slow the time, how heavy the hours
When I am not by thy side
But how they fly when we are close
How weary I am getting with the time between

How shall we live
Since now our very heartbeats are not free?
What future do we see
When there is nothing less but life to give?
We must descend
It is our penance for this love so proud
We two shall weep aloud
Before our silence signifies the end

O earth, lie heavily upon her eyes
Seal her sweet lips, her eyes weary of watching
Lie close around her, leave no room for mirth
With its harsh laughter, not for sound of sighs
Thee hath no questions, thee hath no replies
Hushed in and curtained with blessed earth
Of all the irked thee, from the hour of birth
With stillness that is almost paradise
Darkness more clear than noonday holdeth thee
Silence more musical than song
Even my heart has ceased to stir
Until the morning of eternity
Thy rest shall not end or begin
But when thee wakes again next to me
Thee will think it is not long

Thee are my sun, my moon
Most of all my true north star
Always pointing the way
I must run, run to thee
Memories can never be stolen
Moments such as ours will endure
Kisses are given forever
My heartache this day has never a cure
I will go with thee and be thy guide
In thy most need to be by thy side

Oh, night that joined the lovers
Transfiguring them into each other
That within my throbbing breast
Which for thee entire I save
Lulled by airs that cedars wave
I sank to my rest upon thee
And all thy gifts thee gave
Until every sense was suspended
By thy caresses, all my cares releasing
Thy neck I wounded unthinking
So rapt was I, so swept away
Lost to myself I stayed
My face upon my lover laid

This naked earth is warm with summer
Green grasses, trees, and flowers
Lean to the sun's glorying gaze
Life is colour, warmth, and light
Striving evermore for these
He is dead who cannot see
Or take warmth and light from this glowing earth
Day ends and night enfolds lovers in soft wings

Life had I loved the more
Had it passed away
As quietly and as passionately
Deep and raptured pain
Soothed like gentle rain
My wild tempestuous heart
I am at peace with all
A lonely impulse of delight
I find this tumult in the clouds
In balance, all brought to mind
A waste of breath the years behind
In balance this life, this death

Since there's no help come, let us two kiss and part
And I am glad, yea, glad with all my heart
That thus so cleanly, I myself can free
Shake hands forever, cancel all our vows
And when we meet at any time again
Be not seen in either brow
That we one jot of former love retain
Now at thy last gasp of love's breath
When pulse is failing, passion speechless lays
When faith is kneeling by thy bed of death
And innocence is closing thine eyes
Now if thou wouldst when all have given thee over
Would not thy lover, from death to life bid thee recover

Shall I never hear thee more
By the ready Trent Shore
I do, I do, I do, a calling
Err the early dews be falling
Shall I never hear thy song, all along
Where the sunny Trent floweth
From meadows where wild flowers grow
When the waters winding down
Onwards floweth to the town
Shall I never see thee more?
Where the reeds and rushes quiver and shiver
Stand beside the sobbing river
Sobbing, throbbing, in its falling
To some sandy lonesome shore
Shall I hear thee calling?
Come Jonathan, leave thy grasses mellow
Quit thy primrose and cowslips so yellow
Come Jonathan, rise and follow
Quit thy pipes of parsley hollow, hollow
From thy clovers lift thine head
The wild is calling, calling; come, let us go

Thy summer is burning into mine eyes
I groan at thy indecision
Be less of obligations and more of soul
Pour me out a little peace
And at the end of a tired smile
From thine eyes that see into my night
Enough for me to see

Some words come too late to matter
A phone call never made
A letter put away unanswered
A rendezvous never kept
Recriminations ringing in one's head
When we two have perhaps
Missed our only chance
Words tend to flow too easily
When all time hast gone

I have loved thee in so many ways
In crowds or all alone
When thee were sleeping beside me
When thee were away
I imagined other people with thee
Or worse in other people's arms
I have seen the beach birds and loved thee
I have lost myself to summer and loved thee
Seeing naked trees, the wind raising my collar
Counting lonely minutes until you were there
I have loved thee
I have travelled miles in search of thee
The questions never asked
The answers learnt
Of love's expense, I promised myself
I will not ask where thee were this night
I will only say hello

Sweet closes the even on Burntstump Wood, and blithely awakes the morrow
But the pride of Burntstump Wood can yield to me nothing but sorrow
I see the spreading leaves and flowers, I hear the wild birds singing
But pleasure they have none for me, with care my heart is wringing
I cannot tell, I must not tell, I dare not for thy anger
But my secret love 'twill break my heart, if I conceal it longer
I see thy graceful figure fair, I see thee sweet and bonnie
But, oh, what will be my fate, when thee refuse thy Johnny
To see thee in another's arms, to love, to lay and languish
'twill be my death that will be seen, my heart bursts with anguish
The now sad song of spring wounds my heart with a monotonous languor

My dearest love, would that I had died for thee
Life and this world, hence tedious will be
Nor shall I know what here after to do
If my grief prove tedious too
Silent and sad I walk about this day
As sullen ghosts stalk speechless by
Alas, my treasures is gone, why do I stay
Have ye not seen us walking by?
Was there not a tree we did not know?

The day approaches fast
The day we first loved
And with all my heart, I hope it is not the last
As we walked in Gravelly Hollows
Do not let thy tears, and thy sorrows
Ever keep us apart
For where there is heartache
There must be a heart
Thy voice, thy smile, thy sadness
Thy tears, thy love, I look upon with gladness
Thy love is forever with me
Whatever fortune either of us may possess
The future cannot bring back time

I think I am brave as most in coping with physical pain
I attend to the place promptly or hold my hand over pain
Until the first surprising stab has gone
The body suffers cuts, abrasions, and bruises
Something we can generally see, an inflamed tenderness
But anguish, pain of heart, that interned slow to go
Ache in the midriff that nothing will relieve
Am I brave the? It could be so
Breast pit is Cupid's target, that boy with recurved bow
Who aims at the solar plexus with his barbed benevolent bow
Wears a breastplate then, to blunt and turn his dart
Never, never, I'd rather go forth vulnerable
Than metal my heart away against thee, Brenda dearest

Do thee remember walking in Wollaton Park
In the red sunset of a winter's day?
The grass was a little frosty, snowflakes drifting down
So dark, from an eery sky, I had to go away
'Jonathan,' thee said, 'Johnathan', once again
'Thee grasp my hand, my cold hands within thy own'
Too tightly, yet I did not feel the pain
I could not think or speakMy heart was as stone
How cold it was, my dearest love, how cold, how cold
Now in the long twilight when the sun had fled
The day was dying and the year was old
Why have we wasted so much time, and so to bed
And now the summer trees are full of leaf
Lakes reflect the shining blue above
But still I cannot put away my grief
Nor have I learnt to live without love

Lovely Brenda, blame not me
If on thy beauteous looks I gaze
How can I help it, when I see
Something so charming in thy face?
That liked a bright unclouded sky
Where in the air the sunbeams play
It ravishes my wondering eye
And warms me with pleasing rays
An air so settled, so serene and yet so gay
On all our plains I have not yet seen
In any other nymph but thee
But fate forbids me to design
The mighty conquest of thy breast
For I would rather torture mine
Than rob thee of one moment's rest

Ask nothing more of me, my love
All I can give, thee I give
Heart of my heart, were it more, more would be laid at thy feet
Love that should help to cheer thee, song that should spur thee to soar
All things to me are nothing to give, once to have sense of thee more
To touch thee, and taste of thy sweetness, to breathe thee in is to live
Swept of thy wings as they soar, trodden by chances of thy feet
I have that love, and no more, nothing but love for thee, dearest
He that hath more, then let him give, he that have wings, let him soar
Mine is the heart at thy feet, a heart that must love thee to live

Climbing alone and scorning well-trod paths
He turns his face to the mountains
Shunning all crowds, deep in the far blue heavens
Backing the peaks, crochet shawl of snow
Deep the green forests
Backing the herring bone pattern, its silent, this world
Its hushing long since complete
Where is the power of its stillness?
Trees are still asleep, patterns traced by branches
Exquisite lace in the sky, black is their delicate substance
Perfectly shadowed in the snow
Mantled in white the boughs strain low
Proud of a rare moment's glory, beauty imposed
Parting a wake in new wonder
Soft treading footprints christens new virgin snow
Signing new ways, which eventually the wind will shiver way
Silent this world—its hushing long since complete

Spring of life is sudden, it is her quality
However carefully we watch for her
However long the delay
The strange enchanted green of the winter hedge
The almond blossom, the weeping willow piecing yellow
The laughing daffodil swaying gently in winter's last breath
Like my heart when my dearest is late for our rendezvous
Suddenly thee are there taking thy lover unaware
So beautiful, an exhilarating expectation
Though I stare and stare and stare my fill
Thee keep thy secret still
So sudden is life's spring, be still my soul

O earth, lie heavily upon her eyes
Seal her sweet lips, her eyes weary of watching
Lie close around her, leave no room for mirth
With its harsh laughter, nor for sound of sighs
Thee hath no questions, thee hath no replies

Hushed in and curtained with blessed earth
And all that irked thee, from thy hour of birth
With a stillness that is almost paradise
Darkness more clear than noonday holdeth thee
Silence more musical than any song
Even thy heart has ceased to stir
Until the morning of eternity
Thy rest shall not end or begin
But when thee wake again next to thy lover
Thee will think it is not long
The bond is stronger than before

Strange to walk on this mountain, in the mist and snow
The sky and every stone seem lonesome
No man sees the other, each is alone
For me the world was full of friends while my life was yet light
Truly none are wise who know not the darkness
Inescapably and gently separates him from love
Strange to walk in this mist, life is lonesome
No man knows the other, each is truly alone

Is'nt the wakening earth now to you a purple cape
Uttering first—love's first cry
Vainly renouncing, with a seraph's sigh
Love's natural hope
For meaning earth, foredoomed to perjury
Behold all amorous May
With roses heaped upon her laughing brows
Avoids thee of thy vows
Were it for thee, with warm bosom near
To abide the sharpness of the seraph's sphere
Forget thy foolish words
Go to her summons gay
Thy heart with dead, wing'd innocence filled
Even as a nest with birds
After the old ones by the hawk are killed
Well—dost thou, love to celebrate
The noon of thy soft estuary
Or ever it be too late

I awoke, the sun's rays just barely shining through the early morning mists
Its rays creeping over me and caressing my face
Into my sleepless eyes tenderly
And in that fleeting wistful waking moment
I thought and prayed that the gentle warmth could be there
I turned northwards and took a compass bearing
Sandfield Road, and in my mind, I am looking at thee
Mine eyes felt over the intervening space
My fingers touched thy face
Lean out to meet me
I am bending forward calling with my brain
Do thee not feel me near?
On the wind of thought smiling towards thee
On a lake of mind
Oh, share this moment that never, never may be brought to life again
Once left behind
Alas, I only hear the far-off beating of thy lonely heart
While in between, we two flow the hungry, hurrying waves of time
With the deadly wind blowing us apart
Lovers are no more foreign in their graves
If thee must fade and vanish down the frosty paths of winter

If thee have to go and leave thy lover to this bitter icy chill, I cannot stop thee
Not the flowers of spring from blooming
Or the golden leaves of autumn falling
How could I, it's life's hand that turns the year always
If thee fade into the summer's mists
I will never forget the times we shared
The sunny days, they stand immoral in my mind
Yet they cannot now erase my loneliness
For art thou not my silent tear of joy and madness?

Wildness is my thorny tree
Midnight is my solitude
Living in its self alone
Thy love unfolds a poem to me
Rising like a second moon
On the shadows falls the light
Opening like jessamine
For lovers who love the night
Music for the ears of bats
Silence for the wakeful heart
Sounds that set the heart a dance
Dreams perceive as certainties
The spectral virgin moves into apotheosis
Passionate in abstract chance
Thought becomes the bride of stars
Seeing thee in the distance pass
Beyond my doubting mind
And beyond my heart's distress
Dawn comes measuring and the time of stars
Still are the winds and still the hours
Would it not be peace to lie?
Still in these still hours at my lover's feet
As stars fade from a starry sky
But with hearts another measure beat
Each body wingless as it lies
Sends out its butterfly of night
With delicate wings and jewelled eyes
My love, my beauty, and my poem
The pain is mine, and mine alone
Oh! Gladly love for thee I bear

There is not another that takes thy place in my heart
Yet I suffer from this impediment of the soul
Of being unable to reach out to thee
In my thoughts even on the highest point in this land
Which shrouds me in a ghostly dark grey mist?
Where imaginary figures of souls pass
Flit from rock to rock and mock my most miserable self
In thought the loneliness of these ghosts shout at me
In baffled hurt across the widths of mountains
Above the high-pitched moan of fierce wind
That with bone-bare knuckles upon the subtler vibrations
Of my thought begging heed, begging admittance,
Begging to be heard in this willful yet beautiful mountain wilderness
I hear thee, I heed but cannot reply, being what I am
For I am without key to either of our prisons
And the mountain spaces roll soft and sullen
Between our interlocked souls tossing our vibrations wearily into nowhere
Nowhere in the torment of our being
Do we find a quiet shore to walk upon, and again quietly discover each other
Needless of empty words only the impassioned impeded soul
Stuttering in its cage, stuttering in its rage
Helpless against its very self, raging to be free
For a moment eloquent and free as it was meant to be
Ah! My thoughts unuttered, unutterable thoughts
Broken on their brief doomed career fall limply down the mountainside
Between we two dead as any autumn leave
In any dead season and despair grips my heart upon this mountainside
Waiting to be called home
As called it will be to the hallowed hearts of men
I am tired now, how shall I make it down to the bottom again
Without thy faith, without thy courage, without running to thee
My legs do not want to move
Yet I know I have to summon courage from somewhere
To retrace my weary footsteps
I need not to remember this shadow falling on our summer
Yet the silence between us two is unbearable
Above the grey roar of this mountain wind

I walked alone upon this hill
Where once I walked with thee
Turned my head at highest point
But could not see the view
Though the sun shone bright this day
My eyes were veiled by tears
As I recalled a life gone by
And my last few wasted years
But I walked on and brushed away
Those tears for yesterday
'Life up your heart,' I told myself
Begin your life again today

Time Endears

Time endears
But cannot fade the memories
That love hast made
Though our paths have gone different ways
Thee still reach out
And touch my heart, and I am not alone
Is love not a naked flame
To be gently rekindled
By thy touch or sigh?

Oh, I Love If Only I Had Been Wiser

Have I forgotten, my only love, to love thee
Severed by times all-severing wave?
No! When alone, do my thoughts no longer hover
Over mountains, on that northern shore
Resting their wings where heath and fern leaves cover
Thy noble heart, forever, ever more?
Cold earth and wild December, from those brown hills,
Have melted spring; faithful indeed is the heart that remembers
After much change and suffering
Sweet love, forgive me, no other light, other love has lightened up my heaven,
No second morn has shone for me
All life's bliss from thy dear life was given
All my life's bliss still resides with thee
But when the days of golden dreams have perished
And even despair was powerless to destroy
Then did learn how thy love was cherished
Strengthened and fed without the aid of joy
Then did I check the tears of useless passion
Weaned my soul from yearning after thee, sternly denied this burning wish
To hasten after thee, who was already mine
And yet even yet, I dare not languish
Dare not indulge in memory's rapturous pain
Once drinking deep of that divine anguish
How could I seek love in this empty world again?
Thou art my being, my soul
And what thou art, is life and rest in me

A voice cannot carry the tongue and the lips that gave it wings
Alone must it seek the other
And alone and without its nest shall the eagle fly across the sun
Only another breath will I breathe in this still air
Only one more look cast backwards
And then I shall come to thee
A boundless drop to a boundless sea
Oh! Shall my desires flow like a fountain?
Thy may fill thy cup
Shall it be said that my eve was in truth my dawn?
A seeker of silences am I, and what treasure I find in silences
If this be my day of harvest, in what fields have I sowed my thoughts
And in what unremembered seasons?
If this indeed be the hour in which I life up my lantern
The guardian of the night shall fill it with oil, and he shall light it also
Ever has it been said, love knows not its own depth
Until the hour of separation
And from the mist came a woman whose name was
And she was his lover
He looked upon her with exceeding tenderness
For it was she who had first sought and believed in him
Deep is the longing of your memories and the dwelling place of your desires
Our love will not bind you nor my need to hold you
In your aloneness you have watched our days
In your wakefulness you have listened to the weeping and laughter in our sleep
And he answered when love beckons thee follow him
Though his ways are hard and steep, and when his wings enfold, you
    yield to him
Though the sword hidden among his pinions may wound thee
And when he speaks to you believe him
Though his voice may shatter your dreams
As the north wind lays waste your garden
For even as love crowns you, so shall he crucify you
Even as his, he is for your growth, so he is for your pruning

Even as he ascends to your height and caresses
Yours tender branches that quiver in the sun
So shall he descend to your roots and shake them in their clinging earth
Like sheaths of corn he gathers you up to himself
And threshes you to make you naked
He sifts you to free you from your husks
He grinds you to whiteness
He kneads you so that you are plaint
Then assigns you to his sacred fire
That you may become his bread of life
All these things shall he do unto thee
That you may know the secrets of your heart

But if in your fear you only seek love's pleasure
Then it is better for you to cover your nakedness
And pass out of love's threshing floor
Into a seasonless world where you shall laugh
But not all of your laughter
Weep but not all of your tears
Love gives naught but its self
Love passes not nor would be possessed
For love is sufficient unto love
When thee love, you should not say, 'Love, here is my heart',
But rather, 'Love, I am in your heart.'
And think not that you can direct the course of love
For love, if it finds thee worthy, directs your course
Love has no other desire but to fulfil its self
So if you love and have needs and desires
To melt and to be like a running stream
That sings its melody to the night
To know the pain of too much tenderness
To be wounded by your own understanding of love
And to bleed willingly and joyfully
To wake at dawn with a winged heart
And give thanks for another day of loving
To rest at the noon of day and meditate love's ecstasy
To return home at eventide with gratitude
And then sleep in peace with a prayer for the beloved
In thy heart and a song upon thy lips

Standing on this shore, looking out to sea
At the waves that are hurrying close to me
The tide is turning, the salt water splashes me
I can feel its wetness upon my bare skin
This ocean is calm, its influence prevailing
Helping my mind against the dark thoughts assailing
From deep within, my fears are drifting away
Bringing only the brighter clear ones to stay
Thee have left my side and have gone far away
Another now fills my heart and my mind
Thee have gone across the sea and left me far behind
Now I am alone, and thee are out of reach
I am just a pebble on life's endless beach
Yet within my own heart, I know there is no need for this endless despair
My life is not ended, I must take care
Not to be hurt in this way again
For it only means more anguish more pain
I look out across the sea, and it gives me hope
Its calmness allays my fears and helps me to cope
Mr troubled mind is eased and life will start anew
Just because thee, my love, is lost, I must not remain blue
My thanks to the sea, for with each gentle wave
The thoughts in my mind do not stay grave
Peace and tranquility take over from sadness and pain
Giving me the strength to start living for the day when thee return
This seems so long, times move on, today is here, tomorrow gone
Silent pictures mindless thought, golden memories of thee are caught
Waiting for thee, darling, they'll deliver me far from this deep oceanic sea
To drift no more, we will meet again; the seas uproot all sunken men
I love thee so, please do not weep, farewell no more, no more goodbyes

I do love thee, I do love thee, and when thou are absent, I am sad
I envy the bright blue sky above thee, whose quiet stars may see thee
I do love thee, but I know not why; in my solitude I sigh
That those I do not love are more like thee
When thou are gone, I hate the sound which breaks the lingering
Echo of thy voice, thy voice of music upon my ear
Thy speaking eyes with their deep, bright expressive hue
Between me and midnight heaven arises oftener than my eyes ever knew
I know I love thee, alas others will scarcely trust my heart
And oft I catch them smiling as they pass, because they see me gazing
In the far distance where thou art, yes, I know I love thee

Oh, if love was had for the asking, but love is had by grieving
By choosing and leaving, and there's only thee
To ask me how heavy this heart is
Oh, if love was had for a deep wish in the darkness of night
There would be a truce for longing between dusk and light
But love is had by sighing for living and dying
And there's only thee to ask me how heavy my heart lies
Oh, if love was had for the taking, like honey from the hive
The bees that make the tender stuff could hardly keep alive
But love is a wounded thing, a tremor and a smart
And there's only thee left now to kiss me over my heavy heart

Go now, my love, I too desire it thus
Go swiftly, but you cannot break the chain
Fate has bitter lordship over us, go now in vain
But when thee are in his arms at the dead of night
Safe in the darkness, though thee cannot see
Sudden shall flash upon thy inward sight the form of me
My image will be present in the air
Though thee strive thy weariest to be true
I, thy lover, where the sunrays on the carpet flare
Shall rise for you
Then thee and he together in the spring
At sunset by thy open doorway stand
Shall grow more faint, by too much remembering
My voice, my hand
When he shall bring thee roses, this last hour
I shall snatch thy beauty from thee, like a thief
For there shalt be remembrance in each flower, stem, thorn, and leaf
Slowly, year by year I shall become truer

Until I never leave thee day or night
And shall carefully take my station between thee and all delight
When he shall pass his fingers through thy hair
However gentle thee may be and fond
Thy gaze shall not meet his, thine eyes will stare
At me beyond
Nor will haunt thee, to the verge of death
That when in the bitterness of spirit, he
Shall lean across thee, then thee with thy last breath
Shall call for me
Go now, beloved, but remembering the past
The limits of terrestrial love or hate
I at the portals of the vast unknown
Shall silently wait

Now at the fall of dark, let fall the slatted blind
Shutting the face of fear and all that lies beyond
Out of the house and mind
Now light the friendly lamp and let the kettle sing
In hope his tune may drown the idle chatter
The beat of some dark wing
Now bolt and bar the door and climb the lonely stair
Forgetting if thee can, remembering if thee dare
The long night lurking there

Love, honour, and obey, so it was of yesterday for yesterday
But times have changed, standards blurred
Faith, once sacred, deemed absurd
Lifelong love is an old hat now, unless the bargain is right
With built-in clauses for escape to please the fly by night
Let's set up house before the day, to prove the idea's right
My room is enough to snuggle two, especially at night
And as the years go creeping by, will the ties still hold
Will the sparkling glitter fade, as worthless, false fool's gold?
No matter what you call it nirvana, heaven, bliss
The highs and the lows will always come to strain the patching kiss
The girl or man who once entranced you, may prove in the years

You may prove a different man despite her love and tears
Life shows that man is not foolproof in choosing husbands, wives
And many find their peace at last but in their second lives
Perhaps the ancient wording, should alter just a bit
Achieve a more realistic mood and youthful outlooks fit
Something which would carry through the joys, doubts, and sorrows
Love, honour, and change together, through all our shared tomorrows

Sweet closes the eve on Burntstump Wood
And blithely awakens tomorrow
But the pride of spring in this wood
Can yield nothing but sorrow
I see the spreading leaves and flowers
I hear the wild birds singing
But pleasure they have none for me
Whilst with care my heart is wringing

Oh, to see thee laugh again
That unmistaken sparkle of love in thine eye
I live again. It's joy, it's wealth, it's life itself
Thy lover prays above all
That love, happiness, health
Will always be thine
We emerge from the darkness
The bond betwixt us two
Is stronger than ever

Fragments of thy rich imagining
Splinter and echo within
My heart lifts to the beating of thine
Strung to the pitch of thy demanding beauty
I am resonant to no other touch
That sets my spirit soaring

For this I hold
Friendship is more than life
Longer than love
It shall prove worthier to the spirit
When the body's cold
There is no wisdom that can reach
Truth, if truth can no answer give
The deepest sorrow cannot teach
Thee, my love how to live

Planet drifts out of reach
If I spoke all night, it would be of no use
Thee would not wake and silence my words
Thee would no doubt mistake for ignorance
So sleep, across our window
A small patch of heaven drifts
The stars like sheep are herded
And like satellites' objective time
Circles calendars and marks
These wounds, we think are huge
Sleep—do not be so tense
There is no longer need for barriers
No need of a dumb defence
Thee are understood
This might well be the last
On which there will be any kind of defence
Tomorrow something else
Might wake what has gone to sleep

Perhaps I shall forget thy face
Thy gentleness, thy body's grace
Even your Kimberley accent, deep and slow
May be forgotten, and yet I know
That through the coming years
May love with joy,
May love with tears,
Shall I ever love so well as now?

I was never struck before that hour, with love so sudden and so sweet,
Thy face it blooms like a sweet flower, and stole my heart away complete,
My face must have shown as deadly pale, my legs refused to walk away,
And when thee looked what could I tail, my life seemed to turn to clay,
And then my blood rushed to my face, and took my eyesight quite away,
The fir trees and bushes (dam Bush) around the place, seemed midnight at noon
I could not behold a single thing, words from my eyes did start,
They spoke as chords do from the string, and blood burnt around my heart,
Are all the flowers winter's choice? Is love's bed always snow?
Thee seemed to hear my silent voice, love's appeal to know,
I never saw so sweet a face as that I stood before,
My heart for thee hast left its dwelling place and can return no more.

Last night, ah, yesternight I dreamt that thee were betwixt my thighs,
There thy shadow fell, Brenda, thy breadth was shed,
Upon my soul between the kisses and the wine, I was desolate and sick,
Of wanting thy passion, yeah, I was desolate and bowed my head,
I have been faithful to thee, Brenda, in my fashion,
All night upon my heart I felt thy warm heart beat,
Night long within my arms in love and asleep thee lay,
The kisses of thy red mouth were sweet, but I awoke and found the dawn grey,
I have been faithful to thee, Brenda, in my fashion,
I have forgotten much, Brenda, gone with the wind,
Flung roses, roses riotously with the throng,
Drinking to put thy pale lost lilies out of mind,
But I was desolate and sick for want of thy passion,
Yea, and all the time the dance was long, I hunger for thy lips of my desire,
I cry for madder music and stronger wine, but when the feast is finished,
And all the lamps expire, then falls thy shadow, Brenda, my night is thine,
I have been faithful to thee always in my fashion.

Lay thy sleeping head, my love, upon my faithful breast,
It is true, time and fever burn away individual beauty,
But forever in my arms, till break of day,
Mortal, guilty, but to me entirely beautiful,
Soul and body hath no bounds, to lovers as they lie,
Upon love's enchanted, tolerant slopes,
Not a kiss, not a whisper, or a thought or look to be lost,
Beauty, midnight vision dies, but winds of dawn blow,
Softly around thy dreaming head, such day of sweetness show,
My eye and beating heart will forever always love and bless thee.

Newer dust upon this place is shed,
We stand, see, and hold,
And never cry again,
Under the oak and fir,
We lie, the mountain at our feet,
Waiting on that eternal sunrise
Waiting for thee, dearest Stott Bush.
Jonathan John.

Only For Thee

Gently disarming sleep, sunlight tiptoeing to thy bed,
Taps on thy windowpane, lifts thy drowsy eyelids, and soon,
Soon thee are up and out, drinking deep,
Of a new day's delight, tasting colour smell,
And to feel the cool grass beneath thy toes,
Over a bush where blooms the red rose,
Darkly mysterious to thy virgin sense,
The spider has draped his gossamer shawl, in glittering suspense,
Dissolving shores of light, gems of dew,
Soon to fall, but hear no bell toll,
But to merely look, admire, and be content.

Brenda
Thy name was my grief before, Brenda, the saddest name,
In all the litanies of love and all my letters of flame,
Think of thy poor Jonathan, beloved, and know the blessed pain,
When crusts of love are broken and tears are blossomed rain,
Yet why do I lament the wind that breathes thy name,
The wind of chance that brought me to thee?
To be an offering for my sins my heart held dear,
And though thy passing was for me, the end of something sweet,
Thy name is in my every prayer, thy charm, I meet in every face.

I hide my grief throughout weary days,
When the miles and stubborn nature separate us two,
And gather up the threads of life again,
Remembering thee ever gave thy love to me,
Now, when I feel my courage flicker low,
Thy spirit comes to breathe it into flames,

Until I lift my head and smiling go,
Whispering softly thy beloved name,
And yet it seems but yesterday, when thee were full,
Of childish fears and I would run to thee,
And soothe away, the loneliness of night and dry those tears,
But now thee are the comforter and keep,
From out the shadows, watch, lest I should weep.

My love, thee are the love that comes to me in the dark fields,
In the late night, in the hot breathless dark night,
I love this love we share; in thy arms life is exciting,
Much more than any flirtation with death,
Yet within thy arms, the trees and dark bushes, the soft grass,
And the moon, are not so arrogant as they are when I am alone.

Upon this hearth the fire is red; beneath this roof there is my bed,
But not yet weary are our feet, still round the corner we may meet,
A sudden tree, a sudden stone, that none hath seen but we two alone,
Tree, flowers, grass let them pass, hill and water under sky pass them by
Still around the corner there may wait, a secret gate a new road,
Though we two may pass them by today, tomorrow we may come this way,
And take the hidden paths that run towards the sun,
Home is left behind, the world ahead; there are many paths to tread,
The shadows to the edge of night, until the stars are all alight,
Mist twilight cloud and shade, away shall fade away shall fade,
We'll wander back to heaven and bed, but still around the corner may we meet.

Harebells a blue mist of memory
Of this summer's day
Fragile blue, thoughts with fine threads stem
Holding hanging heads
Curved as remembering curves back
Ghosts of yesteryear which reappear faintly
Bells of clear skies campanile unheard
Now lying alone in bed
I hear the night wind and remember

I'll not weep that thou are leaving me
There's nothing beautiful here
And doubly will the dark grieve me
Whilst thy heart suffers there
I'll not weep because the summer's glory
Must always end in gloom
As following out the happiest love story
Must always close with the tomb
And I am weary of the anguish
Weary to watch the spirit languish
Through dead years of despair
So if a tear when thou art leaving
Should haply fall from me
It is but my heart a sighing

This yearning sorrowing of hopes that lead to strife
I want to see the sky clear, undimmed by its vastness
Or obscured by fear
I want these hands of mine to hold and cherish thee
I want my eyes to see
My feet to speed a million miles
If it should be, to travel by thy side
A sigh with an equal sigh, for nature, cannot outrun herself
That we two should sleep while the world wreaks havoc upon itself
Telling us that our time is done
Then when we awake, tell us, it is undone
For we must start love from the very start again
Maybe somewhere in the corner of my heart
Lies nightmare, futility, and despair
Oh, preach us two no doctrine of chastity, hope, or charity
Preach rather, that our end is near, so that we may make all preparations
To be there, but where?

Sometimes at night, when the moon shines through
I lie in my bed and think of thee
And the shadows of trees away on the wall
And I say to myself I feel nothing at all
Nothing, nothing at all
And yet at night when the moon shines through
I lie in my bed, and think of you
I think no word, no thought, no sigh
As dead men stare with an unblinking eye
I stare at the shadows on the wall
That swing and sway, rise and fall
And I feel nothing at all
Only the moon keeps shining through
Only I can't stop thinking of you
Joy and pain I know will end
But how can nothing ever end
And the shadows sway on my bedroom wall
And I lie in bed and think of thee
And the moonlight bright keeps shining through

Oh someone, someone, hear my call
Stop the moonlight shining through
Stop the shadows on the wall
Oh Brenda, stop me feeling nothing at all

I love thee with such passion now
Is death imminent of love or life?
I love thee so easily, for it is of truth for me
I am afraid at times that God would hardly
Let me know the pleasure of thee
Even for one more day
No man can deserve such happiness
And still walk this good green earth

Thy kiss humid, seal of soft affection
Tenderest pledge of future bliss
Speaking silence my dumb confession
Passions birth, chaste concession
Glowing dawn of a brighter day
When lingering lips, no more must join
What words can speak affection
So thrilling and passionate as thee
When this dawn aches into another day

If I had words as golden as this bush has leaves
And if they took light and shadow in their twist
Then I would let them dance about thy head
Delight thine eyes, caress thy face
Sifting and drifting, to your feet
As my words can never be
Please accept these leaves as substitutes
They are more beautiful than my words

When upon my bed reclining
Buried in the shadow of night
There hovers around me before mine eyes
Thy form of grace and light
As soon as quiet slumber
Hath closed my weary eyes
There softly thy image within my dreams arise
Oh, gather me unto thine arms, and press thy lips, my dear
Close to mine
I want thee to make me warm
When I look into thine eyes
Cold want are soon forgotten
All my earthly troubles fly
But with my dreams at morn
Thy image never fades
For in my heart thee dwell
Through all the livelong day

Thee, my last love, and when it has died
As die at last I know it will
Then shall I seek the warm fireside
Shall tend those plants along my window sill
Read all those books I have been hoarding
Live on memories, grow old with grace
But in this Indian summer, we two hast known
A sunset blaze before love dies
Our love is like an autumn rose
Which opens wide to show its tender heart
Heavy with fragrance as the petals fall
Sweetest of all, my love, sweetest of all

I have a love for thee, wrought of stainless gold
Before thy feet bow, in whose delight, I am content to live
Whose spells of might, are smiles that gleam, tears that glisten
On that fair cheek that blushes if a praise
Warm ripe kisses in the softer hours, when love is perfect
Blossom of sweet flowers are shadow's glances of pure love-light rays
From thine clear brown eyes, wonderful caresses, when love is autumn gold
What other worship can unsurp my days, when I lie amid thy raven tresses
Enraptured by thy smile, though we two are mute
One long calm love, two hearts delight, bright sphere of heaven
Laugh lightly to the silver globe of night that glitters on green fields
Such delight is upon me I would fain sigh into sleep
Until thee, my love, come forth to dream with me, of silent words
Of love and peopled stars where we may live and love and never weep
Nor be weary the shadows creep more on me as I quicken with desire
Lit by thy heart's imperishable fire, have I kept thee long

Say what is love—to live in vain
To live and die and love again
Say what is love—it is to be
In prison yet, yet still be free?
Or seem as free—alone and prove
The hopeless hopes of real love
Does real love on earth cast
'tis like a sunbeam in the mist
That fades and nowhere will remain
And nowhere is air took agai n
Say what is love—a name
A rose leaf on the page of fame

In the evening hour, how still all doth lie
The horned moon shows her face
In the river with the sky
Just by the path on which we pass
Spirit of thee whom I love, whisper to me
Stories of sweet visions as we rove
Here stop and pick with me, sweet flowers
That in this still hour grow
Take them home, but never shake off the dew
Brenda, love sweet spirit of thee
As the bright sun shines tomorrow
Thy dark brown eyes will see these flowers
Gathered by us two in sorrow
In that still hour
When our minds and love were free
To walk alone yet wished I walked with thee

O come, soft rest of cares, come night
Come naked virtues only tire
The reaped harvest of light
Bound up in sheaves of sacred fire
Come nightly and lay thy velvet hand
On glorious days outfacing face
And all thy crowned flames command
For torches to our nuptial grace
Love call us two to arms
Lips our swords are

Once more I hear the music of the lark
Piping clear and shrill
Oh, there it is again my heart
Trilling sweetly shrill
Once more I hear the softness of thy voice
Above the thunder of despair
Confusion, doubt, and folly pass
Leaving our love still fair

For one whole day I have not thought of thee
I have relaxed my longing and my love
Lazed in that timeless haze of the long day though
Walking alone on St Leonard's hill where we two once trod
I finger the sharp pointed leaves clutching at my face
My body soaking in the noonday sun
Living a dream so far from where thee are
Treading a patchwork of sun and shade
Pushing the truth away each waking hour
Dear God, do I believe such lies
When I am remembering naught but thy gentle touch
Thy beautiful form
Remembering thee bending to kiss me
And easing out my pain

To be wounded by your own understanding of love
And to bleed willingly and joyfully
To wake at dawn with winged heart
And give thanks for another day of loving
To rest at noon of day
And meditate on love's ecstasy
To return at eventide
And then to sleep with a song on my lips
That sings the melody into the night
For love is sufficient unto love

No other scene unsurps the wondrous sight
Where stars are diamonds sparkling in the sky
Winter wears a crystal crown this night
Glittering with ice and frost as snow piles high
A quietness for us, as touched all living things
Pure snow drifted, lie deep in ravines and dress
The trees in ermine robes like furry kings
And thought of thy love fills me with happiness
I paused a moment as I turned and gazed upon thee
And to look upon this fairyland of snow
Recalling with nostalgia other times
When icy trees displayed their chandeliers
And now my spirit unbodied, seeks thy lips

Brenda's Dream

I could love life the more
Would it pass away as quietly as the day
Ebbs from the darkening sky
This deeply cherished thought
Deep and ruptured pain
Soothes like the gentle rain
My wild tempestuous heart
To fly above the billowing clouds
And watch the land departing from God's own seat
Is but to die splendidly, but my chosen end
I would humbly creep
As lovers weary for sleep
Pray darkness descends
But should some savage hand my rising womanhood stem
Torn, hunted by this dream from time, lonely to stand,
Life had I loved the more
Had it passed away as quietly as the day
Ebbs from the darkening star,
Day breaks, I awake, and my anxiety returns
The splendid vision has melted away
I am but a woman once more
And now tell me, Jonathan, tell me, my love
Can all this beauty fade with our departing?
No, I am not alone
I have at last emerged from my dream
I am alive, and I must climb to my affirmed goal
I am not alone

The fresh earth in new leaves dressed,
The starry night, autumn evening and morn,
When silver mists are born,
I love snow and all forms of radiant frost,
To share, waves and winds and storms,
Everything which is nature's, all untainted,
By man's misery,
But best of all, I love the tranquil solitude shared,
As is quite and wise and good between thee and me,
What difference but thou dost possess,
These things we seek, we love not less,
I love love, though love hast wings,
And like light canst flee,
But above all other things, dearest Stott Bush,
I love thee—for thou art love and life,

O, differing heart, why is it I tremble when thine eyes,
Thy beautiful eyes, and thy magic voice, draw and stir,
Within my soul this subtle ineradicable longing, for thy tender excitable love,
Is it because I cannot all at once through this half light and phantom-haunted mist
That separates us and enshrouds us from life,
Discern the newness or the strangeness of our paths, nor plumb their depths,
I am like one who comes alone at night, to a strange dream by an unknown ford,
Stands for a moment, yearns and shrinks, being ignorant of thy love,
Though so quiet, it is, so softly murmurous to a so-familiar silvered moon.

From a place I came, that was never in time,
From the beat of a heart that was never in pain,
The sun and moon, the wind and world,
The song and bird, travelled my thought,
Time out of mind, shall I know at last,
Shall I find at last my sweet beginning,
Then tell me death, how long must I sorrow,
My own sorrow, while I remain, the world is ending,
Forests are fading, suns are falling, while I am here,
Now is ending, and in my arms the living are dying,
Oh, shall I not come at last to my lost beginning,
Words are words, they pour through my mind,
Like sand in a shell, the desert's solitude,
Dreams and speculations and vast forgetfulness,
Shall I not learn at last my lost meaning?
Oh, my love, I see thee fly away like a bird,
As fish elude me, as rocks ignore me,
In a tree's maze, thee have closed against me,
The spaces of the earth, prolong in the stars,
Infinite distances, with strange eyes, thee have not known me,
Thy thorns hath wounded me, thy fire hast burnt me,
and thy??? torn me,
How long must I bear this sweet sorrow?
Shall at last find my lost being.

Come to my end softly, on Pavlona feet,
At the greying end of day, into the smoke and heat,
Enter quietly smiling and unknown,
Among the garrulous guests gathered in porters' nests,
To reminisce and moan, come with ornate grief to desecrate my sleep,
But with a calm tenderness togetherness of hands,
Quiet as windless sands, and if thee must weep,
Be it for the old quick lust now lost in the dust,
Remember: *only thee*, could shake it from its lair,
Come softly to my wake and drink and break the ragged crust of friendly bread,
And weep not for me being dead,
But lying stupid there upon a womanless bed,
With sexless stare and no damn thought in my head.

I am losing thee a lover again, all again,
As if thee were mine ever to lose,
The pain is deep, beyond formal possession,
Beyond the fierce frivolity of silent tears,
Absurdly thee came into my world,
My time-wrecked world, absurdly thee leave it now,
As I always foreknew thee would,
I lived on alien joy, thy gentleness disarmed me,
My wine in my barren desert,
Peace across my impassable seas a path of light in my jungle,
Now, as the wind thee go, beyond the wind,
And there is nothing in my world,
Save in the amber dream, the absurdity of that vast improbable joy,
The loveliness, the touch of thee now gone.

Night thoughts, I lie alone, in love,
In a room that no one enters but myself,
Outside in the world I see the trees wave,
In the sky, in the rain, filled with my own life,
Inmate and a prisoner of human walls,

Chairs, books, and pictures, a red rose in a glass,
Are real for me, built in the surrounding space,
For out of life no creature falls,
Only my desire for thee, pierces the lead of my trouble sleep,
The casket of the world, all doors before its beams, crumble and fall,
In its cup carrying my life, my heart passes,
Through walls, through houses, through the air of the time between,
Through dreams and real places,
O never, I pray my heart, seal thy grief,
But go in peace and enter thy love's nest,
Farther than sight can travel and past thought,
O my love, there is no way, my heart is lost,
And tired returns, empty and crying to my breast,
In my darkened room I weep that human love is so,
Blindly must go, and blindly still return,
Lost in the self it knows and lost in the unknown,
Lost for beyond its living life, no human heart may go.

From the South I come to thee, on a stallion shod with fire,
And the winds are left behind, in the speed of my desire,
Under thy window I stand and the midnight hears my cry,
I love thee, I love thee, with a love that shall not die,
Till the sun grows cold and the stars are old,
Look from thy window and see, my passion and my pain,
I lay upon the grass below and faint in disdain
Oh, let the night winds touch thy brow with the heat of my burning sigh,
And melt thee to hear my vow, of a love that shall not die,
Until the leaves of the judgement book unfold,
My steps nightly are driven by the fever in my breast,
To hear thy lattice breathe the word that shalt give me rest,
Open thy door, open thy chamber, and open thy heart,
And my kisses will touch thy lips, of the love that will not fade,
Till the sun grows cold, and the stars grow old,
And the leaves of the judgement book unfold!

Here on this bridge of time, frail entwining,
Between my life and thine we stand and gaze,
Blind to the lightning that about us plays,
And hearing not the eventual thunderclap,
Thee, my love, in thy flower time, I with my diminishing sap,
Condemned to love for a brief few hours or days,
Must always too early go our several ways,
I to a bower not marked upon any map.
Yet from my darkness thee, gone but undestroyed,
I shall attend thee, loving, no word said,
Till thy warm heart, with other love employ,
Does forget me, or consent that I am dead,
Then and only then, shall my ghost, with drooping head,
Turn from thy sight and hurry into that unknown void.

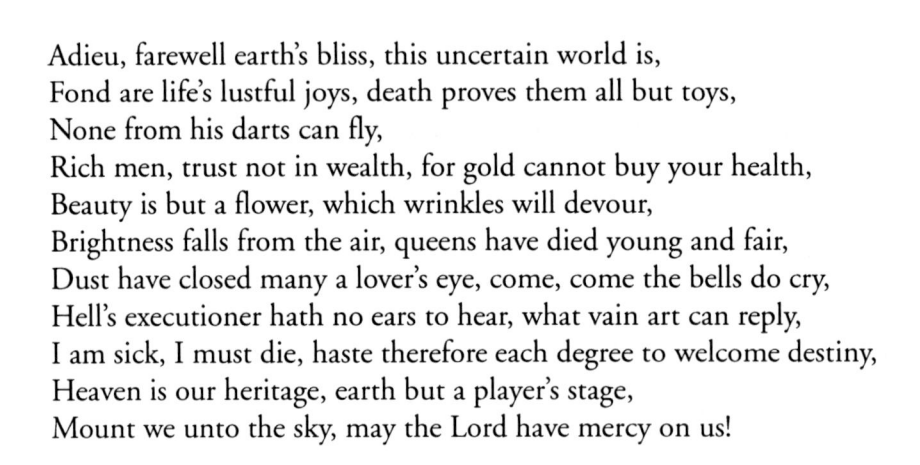

Adieu, farewell earth's bliss, this uncertain world is,
Fond are life's lustful joys, death proves them all but toys,
None from his darts can fly,
Rich men, trust not in wealth, for gold cannot buy your health,
Beauty is but a flower, which wrinkles will devour,
Brightness falls from the air, queens have died young and fair,
Dust have closed many a lover's eye, come, come the bells do cry,
Hell's executioner hath no ears to hear, what vain art can reply,
I am sick, I must die, haste therefore each degree to welcome destiny,
Heaven is our heritage, earth but a player's stage,
Mount we unto the sky, may the Lord have mercy on us!

Dear, if thee should change, I'll never choose again,
Darling, if thee should shrink, I'll never think of love,
Fair one, if thee should fail, I'll judge all beauty vain,
Wise if too weak, more wit I'll never prove,
Dear, sweet, fair wise, change, shrink nor be weak,
And, on my faith, my love of thee will never break,
Earth with all her flowers shall sooner hell adorn,
Heaven her bright stars, through earth dim globe shall move,
Fire, heat shall loose, and frost of flames be born,
Air made to shine, as black as hell shall prove,
Earth, heaven, fire, air, hell, the world transformed shall view,
Ere I prove false to faith, or strange to thee.

My Wearying for Thee

I could be happy, if my heart could rest, as lightly as my head upon thy breast,
I could be happy if my heart could say, 'This is my journey's end', here I will stay,
I could be happy if indeed I knew, whatever stormy path, the last was you,
This would be happiness if this were so and all of heaven, that I'd ask to know,
For this is the dream all humans seek to dream; there is no heart so base,
That does not in the darkness grope, towards this fevered elusive hope,
The smile upon this face, these eyes that shine so bright,
No love's so poor it does not dream, 'tis not a mirage of the night,
It is at last the harbour's beam, dearest of my fitful dreams,
Yonder, the harbour gleams, or so it seems, then why does my heart so tensely rest,
Why does my head but pause upon thy breast, for I could be happy, this at least I know,
If here my heart could rest, and never go! Are sweet dreams of thee my only love?

A Friend is Someone

A friend is someone neither to be leant on, nor lent, lightly that is,
Purer than 'love' itself, for so much of 'love' we know is pride,
So much of friendship is love, in love you ask, no, demand the sky,
And storm at time, in fear, knowing that given time, your love may whittle down,
And leave you with a heap of bones and feet of clay,
That you must treasure fondly and call yesterday, so much for love,
Now for friendship, hands are important as in love, yet somehow different,
The same skin and bones and yet the very feel of them is different,
Friends exchange their hands, neither takes, yet both can give,
And through some mystic side to 'love', you can both part and live,
In 'love' you would most surely die! What is this mystic gift? Even the growth of it,
is as mysterious as love itself; I am a man and would have thee love me,
Now, now, and arrogantly say that I will gladly die when the end comes,
And it will surely come, and yet to really love thee, and have thee truly love me to end
It seems I must deny our love, to call thee friend, yet my heart does not agree,
I both love thee as a friend and as my lover.

Mother, I won't be home this evening, so do not worry, don't report me missing,
Do not drain the canal for me, I've decided to stay alive,
Don't search the woods for me, I'm not hiding,
Just simply gone to get myself classified,
Do not leave out my cornflakes, I'm done with security,
Do not circulate my photograph to society, I have disguised myself as a woman,
And I am giving priority to obscurity, as it suits me fine,
I have taken off my school blazer and put on my jeans,
And now I am going out into the city, so do not worry, do not report me missing,
I've rented a room with no curtains and sit behind the windows growing cold,
Heard your plea on the radio this morning, you sounded sad and strangely old.

The years go slipping through my fingers, the days are long,
The nights are cold, to what avail the dream still lingers,
When the tale is never told, who sees the seed that never flowers,
Who heeds the bell that's never rung?
Who knows of rain but for the showers,
Of music until the song is sung?
The years got slipping through my fingers, as water through a child's grasp,
Mocking the pent-up hopes that linger, silent barren in my grasp.

If ever I saw a blessing in the air, I see it now,
For thee are in my arms, early in this afternoon,
Where brown green the field and hedges drip,
Through sunlight upon the powder of my eye,
Blown bubble film of blue, the sky wraps around,
Weeds of warm light whose every root and rod,
Splutters with brilliant green, and all the world,
Sweats with the bead of summer on its bud,
If ever I heard a blessing, it is here, where birds,
Splash with their hidden wings, tiny drops of sound,
Sounds that break upon my ears, through crests of throbbing air,
Pure in our love as the golden sun dilates, thy lips,
Touch mine, while thee breathe contentedly upon thy lover's breast,
Now as love's passions flame and burn through us two,

Dropping small flames to light thy raven hair,
Now, as my low blood scales to its second chance,
If ever lovers were blest, it is now.

Time is a feathered thing, and whilst I praise,
The sparkling of thy looks, and call them beauteous,
Time takes wing leaving behind him as he flies,
An unperceived dimness in thine eyes,
His minutes, whilst they are told, doth make us old,
And every sand of his fleet glass, increasing age as it does pass,
Insensibly sows wrinkles where flowers and roses did appear,
Whilst we speak, our fire doth into ice expire,
Flames turn to frost, and ere we can love again,
Know how our swan turns crow or how a silver snow,
Springs where love did grow, our fading spring is in dull winter lost,
Since then the night hath hurled darkness, loves shade,
Over its enemy the day, and made the world,
Just a blind hapless, shapeless thing,
As before the light did darkness spring,
Let us two therefore employ its treasure and make shade a pleasure,
Let's number our hours by blisses and count the minutes by our kisses,
Let the heavens new motions feel and by our embraces wheel,
And whilst we try the way by which love doth convey,
Soul unto soul and mingling so makes them such raptures know,
As makes we entranced lie, in mutual ecstasy.

Why Do Thee Not Ring?

Why doesn't she ring? I know we said maybe 1300 hrs or was it half past,
My watch must be fast, why do thee not ring? You're ten minutes late,
I sit by the door, and I'll hear her ring, I've bought thee a rose,
I'll be severe, I'll tell thee. 'My dear, thee must not be late.'
It's now half past one, why doesn't she ring? Why doesn't she ring?
Thee could not forget, perhaps thee are upset, am I in disgrace?
Oh well, if it's that we are both in the wrong, I'll give her the rose,
And say I was wrong, I'll give thee a kiss and say I'm sorry,
Why doesn't she ring? Perhaps thee are ill, I fancied last night,
Thee had a feverish chill, she's lying in bed, she's light in the head,
She's dying, she's dead! Why doesn't she ring?
Thee are tired of me—ah? I've noticed a change; last night thee sounded strange,
So this is the end? Why couldn't thee say? Well, never again!
Thee need not explain, I know who it is! I've done with thee now,
Why doesn't she ring, its now half past, well never again!
I'll send her the rose, she'd laugh I suppose! A flirt, a fraud,
I'll travel abroad. I'll go to the East, I'll shoot wild beast,
And now for a drink, I'll have a stiff drink, brandy, I think,
And drown myself in it. I'll shoot myself . . . oh,
how I love thee!—'Hullo!' What late not a minute,
No! I've just come in, thee sound wonderful,
Thee said you would ring.

Oh, wild gladness of the waiting spirit,
Which hears, like music on distant horn,
The first sweet notes, silver notes of coming rapture,
The music of love as yet unborn,
Which trembles at a lover's touch, whoever the giver,
Or springs at the sight of love, unto full flower,
Or prays in purity with fingers folded,
For consummation of its waited hour,
Which rising when the East light is flooded,
Stands silent with expectant arms outflung,
To greet the sun unrisen, the red unbudded rose,
The book unopened, the song unsung,
False, fooling hopes of ecstasy eternal!
The enraptured moment of love's come, is grasped, is gone,
Yet through the lengthening years we seek it ever,
And youth remembering drives us two on.

One thousand oaths, your fears perhaps will not remove
And if I gazed a thousand years into thine eyes
I would no deeper love thee than this moment
It is not nor ever will be in our power
To say how long will love last
It may be within this hour that we lose these joys
We have lasted these many years
The blessed that mortal be, from change in love are only free
Then blessed since we mortal lovers are
Let us not ask how long our love will last
But while it does, let us take care
Each second be with pleasure passed
Would it not be madness to deny to live
Because we are sure to die?
Our weeping, laughter, love, desire, and hate are not long
Out of a misty dream, our paths have emerged for a while
They will all close within that dream

Always in love, The having worth the losing
When loss means pain, not withering, not refusing
It's a terrible price from the beginning
Though we two lovers, born for permanence
A state where time is ample, and not time
With joys enough to fill a river, but not running
I see a sunray like a summer fly
All those wild minutes when thee have lain with me
Dance on thy beautiful face, through sheltering trees
And tease a rainbow within thine eyes
And sliding down from cheek to die out in moss
Then it's time for goodbye
As earth comes back with the first shadow of night
I'd not exchange thee that tiny death of light
For centuries of unvarying happiness

Darling of my heart here in this room, thee are out side this room,
Here in this body thine eyes drift away, least of this world,
Yet thee are most of this world,
Today this moment, when those who would have we two hide our love,
In dreams of painted of unfilled desire, hate triumphing outside,
Where the brave who live and love are hurled through flood waters shot with fire,
So be it, I must bear thy absence, next to my heart where others wear their love,
Indeed thee are my love, my link with life,
All in life we knew, thine eyes hold still, shadows within which bells are tolled,
Yea, I look into those deep brown eyes, shafts of pleasure to my heart,
Which cannot take part in lies, of acting these gay parts,
Under our lips, our minds become one with weeping, through sleep though unsleeping,
Oh! What is the use of weeping, at the root of thy life, all it can prove
Is that, the extremes of love reach out and panic fills the night in which we are alo
Yet my grief for thee, is myself, a dream that tomorrow's light will sweep away,
It does not wake day after day,

The final act of love, my dearest, is not of dove twining neck with dove,
Oh no, it is the wild storm fruit, sperm of tangling distress,
Fingernail tearing at dry root, thy deprived, fanatic lover, naked in the desert,
Of all except his heart, in his abandon must cover, with wild lips and torn hands,
With a blanket made from his own hair, with comfort made from his own despair,
My sexless corpse laid in the sands, pursuing that narrow path,
That path, how far we both hath travelled, sweetheart,
Since that day when we first chose each other as each other's rose,
And put all other's worlds apart,
Now we assume the coarseness of lovers, where all are all and all alone,
And to love means to bless each other, dearest and nearest lover,
No word can turn the day or the freezing night of silence, where all our dawns delay,
Yet we learn to love with singleness of mind, as with regret stronger passions hold,
All those past doubts of life one happiness does prove,
Better in death to know the happiness we lose than die in life meaningless,
Misery of those who lay beside chosen companions, they never chose.
Now I lay awake at night, I seldom dream, but lately, I see thy slender figure stand,
In russet black ready-made, thy hand held some limp daisies tight.

Thee gaze along the meadow by the Trent so intent, thee were so sad to me as I slept
I thought I heard thee sob or cry aloud, but thee only gazed along the meadow's brim,
Alas, I awoke and found that it was I who wept.

The bird has chosen, and the world of spring under lover's banner is enrolled
But thou, chained to the iron couch of wedlock fast, are mourning,
While or else in nature dost sing the deep delights of love,
Still on thy brow, lurks the dark shade, thy smile is overcast,
With fear of the worlds thought, and lips of love, pale at the spectre,
Imminent, immense, cold chastity, the child of impotence,
And eyes grow dim with grey distrust thereof, forget,
Forget dear heart, life's glow is sweet, come to thy lover's arms that grow divine,
At the first eloquence embrace of thine, while pulses in wild unison warmly beat,
Come now, to the valley that I know, walled with glistening steep,
Filled with green lawns and forests of black pine,
Where the clear streams shall sing us two to sleep, with their murmuring,
A divine device, come with me there, and we shall surely twine,
To hold my love and lead my kisses on, from night to night upon our purple bed,
We will forget in love the world of tears, whose tumult reaches not our amorous ears
Come with me then, let chaster snow blush our sunset when our limbs grow fain,
To twine in close caressing, let it blush, redder at sunrise, when our eyelids grow
Weary of kissing and our arms again slowly unclasp and our fair cheeks do flush,

With memory's modesty, ah, the mountains glow, warmer and whiter,
Dreamland's power shall wane, while the sun tints the beauty of the bush, (balls)
And the forest with his fingertips of budding fire and we surprised shall wake,
While shadows brush in the darker colour and roam our valley,
Fresh delicate delight, with smiling lips, sweet with green sward,
Faint flower and tender tree, there all winter may we lay and idly dream,
Still of our love and there forgetfulness of past sorrow that may steal o'er thy brow,
In this new birth of stainless happiness, rich harvest of the blossoms of desire,
Satisfy our passionate needs, yet forever fresh, in our hearts,
And there may'est thou love to thy fullness nor ever tire,
Of linking thy lover with thy dainty mesh of raven ripples of delicious fire,
Doubt not, dear love, nor hesitate to say, but blush if thou wilt,
I love to see thy cheek grow hot with the thoughts of love,
Let the word be said, between we two whisper me yes! forget thy Peter
My soul will leap to hear, as thine to speak, love forget thy loveless bed,
And the cruel wreck of thy dear life on wedlock's piteous sands,
Love, all in all, link on golden bands, forged in heaven without thaw or fleck,
Thy sudden passion burns upon my cheek, thy heart clings to me a perfect 'yes'.

One Withered Leaf

One withered leaf—I enclose and everyone knows: Autumn,
The windows rattle shiveringly at night, O, green world,
How ostentatiously you change your colour!
Already winter is rustling among the leaves, and all of a sudden, the
   birds have go
Like last fruits their songs dropped from the tree,
Now the wind dwells in the branches
The old people in the park bow their heads still lower,
Even lovers are silent; soon all the boats will be in harbour,
The swans on the pond sleep in misty light,
Summer—a dream flown away, and spring—what a fabulous distant rumour!
A withered leaf is blown silently into the air,
And all know autumn.

Newer dust upon this place is shed
We stand alone and see
And hold and never to cry again
Under the grass and shadow of this church he lies
And all of Kimberley at his feet
Waits the eternal sunrise

Why! Why, tell thy lover
Bliss he must never enjoy
Why! Why undeceive him
And give all his hopes a lie
Oh: why while fancy slumbers
Raptures, why wouldst thou be so cruel?
Wake thy lover from his dream
Now as tinted clouds cross the sun
Like so many golden fleeced sheep
Winding their way wearily home
Midst the dying day
My thoughts also turn homewards
But, although my home is full of bright light
And warm to keep out the cold
Long, lonely nights
My life lacks a precious being
A warm and very beautiful person—thee
I love thee, I love thee
For what might have been
As well as what was to come

Under trees on gravelled paths
Leaves intertwine with the wind
Sounding like the brisk footfalls of autumn
Fading as now winter creeps in
Only we two lovers are seen in the park
Breath misting on frosty air, whispering happily
As hand in hand.
We wander aimlessly amongst the leaves

Seasons come and go
Time changes many things
But my love for thee
The dearest, most important in all the world
And I will go on caring
Just the same my whole life through
Time cannot change my love
Fir it belongs only to thee
There will be of course daffodils again
Looking for all lovers like telephones
Waiting to be buzzed in by all the usual bees

My love, we grow older
And admit to wishing upon a star
We will wake up to find our pillows, wet with tears
When in the loneliness of our lives apart
This always leads back to ourselves
Or when at night, we turn over
But only to find the bed too wide
Is it not that we see the stars
Sail slowly through the night
And wish that we were closer

I watch a solitary leaf torn by high winds
From a tree stark naked against the night sky
It whirls helplessly and not belonging to the ground
My shoulders grow cold, thee wrap a cover around
And we two are warm
Nothing else outside this room exists
We relax the vigil against our realities
And silently, without trying, we drift
On waves of ecstasy into the sanctuary of dreams
'tis again time for lovers to part
Our hearts grow cold, a solitary snowflake
Drifts slowly down through the clear night sky

Lover

A friend is someone neither to be learned on of lent
Lightly that is
Purer than love itself
For so much of love we know
Is pride, so much of friendship, love
In love you ask—no demand the sky
And storm at time in fear
Knowing, that given time
Your love may whittle down
And leave you with a heap of bones
And feet of clay
That you first treasure fondly and call yesterday
So much for love
Now for a friend
Hands are important as in love
Yet somehow different, the same skin and bones
And yet the skin of them feel different
Friends exchange their hands
Neither takes, yet both can give
And through some mystic side of love
You can both part and live
In love you must surely die
What is this mystic gift?
Even the growth of it is as mysterious as love itself
I am a man, and would have thee love me
And would arrogantly say that I would die for thee
When the end comes, and come it will

If thee should leave me in days to come
Grant that this may not be so, but if it be so
Your love for me must fade I know
You will remember, and you will forget
But oh, imperishable strong
My love for thee shall burn and glow
Deep in your heart, your whole life through
Unknown, unseen but living bliss
So shall thee bear with me
With all your living days
Forget then what thee will
But not my love for you
Remember this if thee shall not return

I want to eat this greedy seed of life
These yearnings, sorrowing hopes that lead to strife
I want to see the heavens clear
Undimmed by vastness, or obscured by fear
I want to use these hands of mine
To hold and cherish whatever is
I want for us my eyes to see
My feet speed a million miles, if it should be
A sigh should want an equal sigh
For nature cannot outrun itself
That we the casual passers-by
Should sleep while nature wreaks her havoc on us
Telling us our time is done
Then when we wake, tell us it is all undone
And to start again
In my corner of the square, lies nightmare
Next to her, for closest kin, futility
And next to her despair
Preach me no doctrines of chastity, hope of charity
Preach me rather that the end is near
I will comfort my Lord
And make all the preparations there

This day is done and darkness falls
On the wings of the night
As a feather is wafted downwards
From an eagle in flight
I see thy face gleam through the mist of my eye
And a feeling of sadness comes over me
That my soul can resist
A longing that's not akin to pain
Come, read me some poem, my love
And the night shall be filled with music
And the cares that infest the day
Shall fold their tents
Like the Arabs and silently steal away

First, last and dearest love, my own
Thee best beloved, thee love alone
Once and forever, so I love thee
A smile because nights are short
And every morning brings pleasure

So green was our leaf this year
Sweet all our tender grief, there was no fear
For never was there any spring as our spring
My heart always slow in learning, found content in thee
No feverish thing our love, but gentle, deep, and dear
Summer is now dead and sorrow spent
Oh my darling, Stott Bush, take me by the hand
Help me understand the winter that I see drawing near

Thy spirit calls me home
I feel no stranger here
Did I not lean my head against stone pillars raised
By hands long since dead
And pray for some power
To carry me to thee, to thy arms
In pursuit always my aim
Pursuit of a dream that eludes
Pursuit of thee, it is the only cure that cures

Sigh for my burning desires
So let us two gather while it still hath worth
The rose of love that ne'er will bloom again

Here on the bridge of time,
Frail overlap between my life and thine
We stand and gaze
Blind to the lighting that plays around us
And hearing not the eventual thunderclap
Thee in thy flower time
I with my diminishing sap
Condemned to love
For a few brief hours or days
Must always too early go our separate ways

But Brenda, I know that I will stand
Some day in the loneliest wilderness
Sometime my heart will cry
For the soul that has been
But that now is scattered to the winds
Deceased, devoid
I know that I will wonder
Will utter a cry
O beautiful Brenda, the woman I love
Oh, wither hath thee gone
But I will not give thee my soul

Thy Jonathan is thy changeless lover
His love surrounds thee ever
Forget thyself and all the world
Put out each burning light
The stars of love are watching overhead
Sleep softly then, my love goodnight

Entranced my thoughts of thee
I climb no mountain, travel along no track
As the evening selva oscura approaches
Fleeting away beneath us two

Poems Ruled By the Heart

Once more I hear the softness of your voice
Above the thunder of despair
Confusion, doubt, and folly pass, leaving out love still fair
Forever, ever will I hear the lark
And see thee gathering roses in the dark

Slender hairs cast shadows though but small
Seas have their source and so have springs
The dial stirs, yet none perceives it move
The firm faith is found in fewest words
True hearts have ears and eyes
Yet no tongue to speak
The hear they see and sigh they may brea k
And love is love in beggars and in kings
Thy Jonathan, cannot sing, but I love only thee

The years will mark the face
And sorrow strains the heart
But only the young can lose the race
For the old no longer take part
In youth or age there's little to choose
And tears are the common cost
For whether you sigh at close of day
Or sigh at the break of dawn
There are tears for what you pray
And tears for what hast gone

And when this earth has turned to dust
That the blood and tears of our love shall be true
We will wander through pits of fallen stars
Searching for each other and showing our hearts
As tokens of our love to the seeingless eye of space
So in the blistering day of truth
Where among the lonely speechless stars
We wonder, bereft of these dear senses we know
Unable to communicate, we may yet be there
But where? We will not forget to be near heaven
Did our love comply?

O, those who never have aspired
To ride the clouds unfurled
Of what use is life,
Of what use is their world?
There are two lives, the one when light first strikes a new awakened sense
The other when two souls unite
And we must count our life from thence
When you loved me and I loved thee
Then both of us were born anew
Love then to us new souls doth give
And in these souls did plant new powers
Since when another life we live
The breath we breathe is not ours
Love makes those young when age doth chill
And when he finds the young keeps young still

In this fair stranger's eyes of brown
Thine eyes, my love, I see
I shiver, for the passing days
Hath borne me far from thee
This curse of life, that not
A nobler, calmer train
Of wiser thoughts and feelings blot
Our passions from our brains
But each day brings pretty dust
Our soon choked souls to fill
And we forget because we must
And not because we will
I struggle towards the light and thee
While the night is chill
Upon times barren, stormy flow
Stay with me, Brenda, still

Sweet twining hedge flowers, wind stirred in no wise way
On this April day
And hands that cling in hand, still glades and meeting faces scarcely framed
A muddy path that draws the moonlight skies deep to its heart
And mirrored eyes fresh hourly wandered over
This moonlight wood of light and cloud
Two souls softly spanned as one
Near heaven of smiles and sighs our bodies leant unto each other
Visible sweetness our passionate hearts
Learn by love's degree
As on this spring day the clouds and moon did rest
Upon this wood and love, remember dearest

Own the sweet season, each thing as it may
Thoughts of strange kindness and forgotten peace
In me increase, and the tears within me arise
Within my happy, happy mistress's eyes
And lo, her lips averted from my kiss
Ask from lover's bounty, ah, much more bliss
Isn't the sequestering and exceeding sweet?
Of dear desire electing his defeat
Isn't the waked earth now to thee purpling cope
Uttering first, love's first cry
Vainly renouncing with a seraph's sigh
Love's natural hope?
Fair-meaning earth, foredoomed to perjury
Behold, all amorous May
With roses heaped upon her laughing brow
Avoids thee of thy vows
Were it for thee, with warm bosom near
To abide the sharpness of the seraph's sphere?
Forget thy foolish words, go to her summons gay
Thy heart with dead winged innocence filled
Even as a nest with birds
After the old ones by the hawk are killed
Well, dist thou, love to celebrate
The noon of thy soft ecstasy
For it be too late
Or e'er the snowdrops die
Yes, in me increase this strange kindness and forgotten peace
And tears arise, at the thought of my lover's happy eyes

Joy fills our cup that flashes clear
The year fades a whisper now
Shadow and silence are our throng
The seasons—we are happy here
'tis autumn and the dying breeze
Murmurs, embrace the moon replies
Embrace to soughing of the trees
Calls us two to linger lover wise
And drain our passion to the lees
The beeches bash themselves to kiss the skies above
As I kiss thee
Leave us, sweet autumn, to our love

We look from out of the shadows
On through future years
For the soul would have no rainbows
Had the eye no tears

I shall not die, but live
Before thy face I stand
Jonathan, for thou called me so
All that I have, I bring all, all I have, I give
Oh my love, now let thy judgement stand
Smile them, and I shall sing
And not question thy judgement

Because I love thee,
more than it suits man to say
I have displeased thee
Now should thee put this world between us
And should we part stiff and dry
If here where clover whitens on yon hill
And no tall flowers to meet thee
Stirs in free foiled grass
Halt by our lanes of happiness
Joining this heart that no longer stirs
Say Jonathan that loves thee
Was one who kept his word

When the breath of twilight blows flame to misty sky
All its vapours sapphire, violet glow and silver gleam
With there magic flood we two, through the gateway of thine eyes
And we are one with twilight dreams
Full of peace, sleep, and dreams in this vast quietude
We are indeed one with our hearts at rest

Whether, my love, I find thee bright and fair
Or still as bright as thy raven hair
With equal grace thy tresses shine
Ah, my queen, my love is for thee in my heart
Love to thee will dwell divine
In these thy locks on that far day
When thy raven hair turns to grey

Thee my last love and when it has died
As die, alast I know it will
Then shall I seek the warm fireside
Shall tend those plants along my windowsill
Read all those books I have been hoarding
Live on memories, grow old with grace
 But in this Indian summer, we two hast known
A sunset blaze before loves dies
Our love is like an autumn rose
Which opens wide to show its tender heart
Heavy with fragrance as its petals fall
Sweetest of all my love, sweetest of all

Thee will not ask, perhaps, wherefore I stay
Loving thee so much so long away
Oh, do not think, 'twas I did part
It was my body, not my heart
For like a compass, on thy love
One foot is fixed and cannot move
The other may follow the blind
Guide of giddy fortune, but not slide
Beyond thy service not dare venture
To wander far from thee, the centre

When in the darkness of night remorse returns to haunt me,
And beat incessant drums inside my head,
And grief wells up inside me for love not given,
Lack of sympathy for those now dead,
Then, in the darkness, as I lie unsleeping,
Lost in the depths of that three o'clock despair,
The age-old cry comes to my mind unbidden,
'Show me, O Brenda, show me that thee are there.'
But now the greyness creeps in behind the curtains,
Birds awaken while it is still night,
Blackbird, thrush, and linnet, singing to greet the light,
High as the highest bell within the belfry,
In crystalline cascades of brilliant notes,
This chorus of the dawn, perfect in beauty,
Rises in rapture from beating throats,
And as the chilly air blows through the window,
The sun leaps upwards into a yellow misty glow,
The last clear trembling voice calls silence,
And I am answered now, yes, I do know,
That as daylight strengthens, the black dreams of the night are borne away,
I draw back my curtain, and hope is with me to begin this day,
And the longing and deep burning desire to sense thy fragrance
like woods after rain,
To see and hold thy slender form again,
I start, I awake from my daydreams—time with impatient hands,
Has again snatched thee from my mind, O when, my love, O when, my love.

We would sit down and think which way,
To walk and pass our long love's day,
My love to grow, vaster than the universe, and more slow.
One hundred years would go to praise,
Thine eyes, and on thy forehead gaze,
Two hundred more to adore each lovely breast,
But thirty thousand more to the rest,
An age at least to every part.
And the last age to show thy heart,
For Brenda Stott Bush, thee deserve this state.

The sky is overcast,
With a continuous cloud of texture close,
Heavy, all whitened by the moon,
Which through that is indistinctly seen,
A dull, contracted circle, yielding light,
So feebly spread that not a shadow falls,
Chequering the ground from rock, plant, tree, and tower,
At length a pleasant instant gleam, stars perceive,
And startles the pensive lovers, where they tread,
Their lonesome path, with unobserving eye,
Bent earthwards, they look up—the clouds are split asunder,
And above their heads they see,
The clear moon, and the glory of the heavens,
There in a black, vaulted heaven she sails along,
Followed by a multitude of stars,
How fast they wheel away—yet vanish not,
But they are silent, still as they roll along,
Immeasurably distant in that blue, black vault of the universe,
Built around by those white clouds,
Which deepen still, its unfathomable depth,
At length the vision closes, to lovers' eyes,
and the mind is not disturbed by the delight it feels,
Which slowly settles into peaceful calm,
Lovers who are left to muse upon this solemn scene.

The years go slipping through my fingers
The days are long, the nights are cold
To what avail the dream still lingers
When the tale is never told
Who sees a seed that never flowers,
Who heeds a bell that is never rung,
Who knows the rain,
But for the showers,
Of music until the song is sung?
The years go slipping through my fingers
As water through a small child's grasp
Mocking the pent-up hope that lingers
Silent, barren in my clasp
I've bought these bright tears with heartbreak
But this is what I have chosen
This moment so bitter so free
The years go slipping through my fingers
From so much that was offered me

At times we use harsh words
To correct, or impose our view
The error of one's ways, perhaps
Yes, such action may be
Our tongue can be the flames of fire
And burn the heart of mankind
Even our tone of voice can hurt
If not used with thought behind
Loving thoughts we wish to pronounce
Are expressed in the selfsame way
And if our hearts possess love
Love will know what we say
So, prior to speaking or writing,
Let us think
Of what lies within our hearts
And if our tongue is full of love or fire
All ill thoughts from us should part

I did not make the conditions of life, love whereby
The laws of the stars will never change, though I
Said, 'God give me to love' or I will die
I am not wise yet, why must I know so much
That teaches me what I can never learn
That I can put my trust in thee, my love
The solid earth and extensive sky
Are flimsy and impermanent as I
My earth, my love, my thoughts will die within me
Oh, lovely earth, with richer life than mine
Whose teeming seas and blooming fields decline
Slowly towards stillness, yet remain
For animals shall fly the secret plains
And human greatness suffer great pains
Thy shrinking form, broken forgetful face
Thy cooling heart all lies lifeless, cold
Shall thy hot blood and conscience grief cool?
If so, then all forest burn in their own funeral pyre

Darker than eyes shut in a darkened room
Colder that the coldest hours before the dawn
My nightmare body leaves its bed to walk
Across an unseen lawn
Where unseen objects nudge my bare feet
They force a shout within my throat
Which struggling cannot get out
I awake the dream is over
No one is standing beside me now, nor has there been
Thee lie beside me, while I count the things tomorrow will bring
In idleness, commission, or false choice
In a lack of purpose or uncertain voice
You sleep, and in the darkness, I hear thee breathe
Though uncertainties and responsibilities
Some time thee tell me of thy own strange dreams
Mine are banalities
Trudging down trodden paths to find a heap
Of fragmented, unromanticised by sleep
Letters unwritten upon my desk
Of money, my age, things I would not have said
Give me time to decide, I stifle in bed
Searching for names to call it by
This blackness that comes down finally
But names are nothing, dreams are nothing

Thee do not appear
Nowhere down all the mazed days of my searching
In this autumnal spring of sorrow
Thee stepped smiling and sure
Out of the walled garden of my heart
To some improbable tomorrow
My heart knows thee still most intimately
Roots run deep in my garden
Though I may miss thy face in a crowd
Joy played awhile with my dreams
Thee gravely gathered them up in a shroud
A little time of pleasure
But mine while time is known
Now only this I know
That wherever thee are in time
By whosoever loved, my heart will go
Still capable of song
The faint and ineffable
As fragrant as frost
Thee taught me a thing of such moment
I did not know one could live
With life itself lost

When love and beauty wander away
And when there's no more hearts to be sought
When the old earth limps on through another weary day
And the work of the seasons cries undone
Ah! What shall we do for a song to sing?
We who have known love, beauty, and spring
When love and beauty wander away
And pale fear lies on the cheeks of youth
And we live in or at the end of the world's untruths
Oh! What shall we do for a heart to prove?
We who have known beauty, spring, and love
Can you imagine this happening to us two?
Oh, thou art my love,
Whose kiss upon my lips still seems the first kiss
Thee, whose summoning eyes
Even now this moment, show me each day
Love's world is a new sunrise every dawn
Thy touch is like a hand softly laid upon my soul
Those tired eyes at times that my oath has the keeping of
What word can answer thy word?
What gaze to thine which now absorbs me within its shore
Thy beautiful eye holds me until I am mirrored there
What embrace, thy kiss my innermost heart
Beloved and lovely, my love

The ferns and leaves of green made a garland for thy hair
The warm-scented air was all around us two and above
My head was spinning, my senses reeling my thoughts were all of thee
In the quick sands of my mind thee always come to me in wonder
And speak of faraway lands, whilst all around us echoes still
The whispering of the wind, thee came, my dearest Brenda
Out of the deep oceans of my mind, thy warm skin, they beautiful body
We walked on the clouds of the seventh dawn, thee trembled
And my soul was laid bare; we came as one, and the still air was silent
My senses rode on the wings of an eagle. I lost all sense of time
But suddenly, thee left thy lover, to walk in the loneliness of my mind

My pillow of fern gazes upon me this night
Empty my heart as a gravestone
I never thought it would be so bitter to be alone
Not to lie down asleep in thy hair
I now lie alone in this silent wood
The moon darkened by fleeting clouds
And gently stretch out my hands to gather in thine
Softly press my warm mouth against thine and towards thee
And kiss myself exhausted, suddenly to become wide awake
All around me the night grows still
The stars between the trees shine clearly
Where is thy sweet mouth, where is thy raven hair?
Oh, how I drink the pain in every joyous memory

Above the edge of the darkest dark, will always appear the first lances
    of the sun
Along our mountains and ridges will the sun's rosy heralds run
Where all the vapours of the morning down the valley go
Like broken armies, dark and low
Look forward our two hearts, from every hill
In folds of life our violets and daffodil
The sunrise banner flow
Oh, fly away on silent wing, ye gloomy owls of night
Oh, welcome little birds that sing in coming light
For new, and new, and ever new
The golden bud within the blue
And every morning of our love seems to say
There's something happy for us two on the way

Love me, darling, with all your heart, feeling, thinking, seeing
Love me in the lightest part, love me in full being
Love me with thy open youth, in its frank surrender
Love me with the vowing of thy mouth, within its silence tender
Love me in thy gorgeous airs, when the world has crowned thee
Love me kneeling at thy prayer, with the Lord around thee
Love me pure as musers do, up upon the woodlands shady
Love me gaily, sure and true, my beloved lady

In the peaceful sunlight of sleep
Is the pleasured night of spirit and flesh?
Made one, thy hand found my hand, leaf shape of bone
The strong interstices measured knowing, as instantly known
Our lips say little, nothing of any consequence
But what each hand beat out, in time with our pulsing hearts
Came clear enough for us two to sense
This, said one hand, is true, this is true beyond doubt
Out of the whirlwind of time in the cold night of stars
Our hand shapes to each, this and the knowledge of this
Our ears on the pillow heard
But being sun drenched with sleep and conscious of nothing amiss
There was no need for words
Just this—this—this our love

Kiss
No whisper, scarce a breath
But lips gentle, to drain sweetest passion
Scarce a sigh beats the dead hours out
Scarce a melody
Of measured pulses quickened blood of desire
Which pours its deadly flood through soul and shaken body
Scarce a thought but sense through spirit
Most divinely wrought to perfect feeling
Only through lips' electric ardour kindles
Slips through the circle to thy lips
To drain all pleasure in one draught
No whispered sigh, no change of breast
Love's a posture perfectly, once gained no more
The fever grows hotter or cooler as the night wind blows
Fresh gusts of passion in waves of frenzy
Concentrate out thirsty mouths
On that drinking cup, whence we suck sweet nectar up
Too often too hard fresh fires invade our veins
And unquiet shades of night made noises in the darken room
Yet did I raise my head and behold thine eyes red as fire
A tigress maddened with supreme desire
White arms clasped me a fervent breast that glides about my breast
Thy fevered mouth gentle crimson red
A very beast of prey and I love thee
Fiery weary, as thou art of me
But raises no head. I know thee
Breast and thigh, lips and mouth
??? me o'er that gate of death

We part, but by these precious drops
That fill thy lovely brown-green eyes
No other light shall guide my steps
Till thy bright eyes rise again
Thy the fairest of all thy sex
Hast bless my glorious day
Thee alone shall my shining planet fix
As I tread the weary path to the dark unknown

Raving winds around her blowing
Yellow leaves the woodlands strewing
By the Trent hoarsely roaring
Bren the strayed deploying
Farewell hours that late did measure
Sunshine days of joys and pleasure
Hail thou gloomy night of sorrow
Cheerless night that knows no tomorrow
O'er the past too fondly wandering

Nor concrete, nor gilded monuments of princes
Shall outlive my words
For thee shall shine in mine eyes more than these things
Unswept stone, besmeared with the smuts of time
When wasteful wars shall statues overturn and masonry tumble
Nor mars his sword, nor wars quick-fires shall burn
The living record of my love, against death and all oblivious enmity
Shall I pace forth thy praise and still find room
Even in the eyes of posterity
That wear out this world to ending doom
So, till the judgement that thyself arises, thee, my love
Will live in this heart of mine and dwell forever in thy lover's eyes

Thee took my heart in thy hand, O my love, O my love
I said, 'Let it fall or stand, let me live or die.'
But this once hear me speak, yet a man's words are weak
Thee took my heart in thy hand with a friendly smile
With a critical eye, thee scanned, then set it down
And said, 'It is still unripe, better wait awhile.'
Wait for the skylarks to pipe, till the corn turns brown
And as thee set it down it broke, broke but I did not wince
I smiled at the speech thee spoke, at the judgement I heard
But since I have not often smiled or questioned since
Nor cared for cornflowers wild, not sung with the singing bird
Thee took my heart in thy hand, my broken heart thou hast seen
Judge thou was, my hope written in sand, O my love, O my love
So let thou judgement stand, yes, judge me now this condemned of men
This marred heedless day, take thou this to see
Scan this my heart, both within and without, refine with fire its gold
Purge thou its dross away, yes, hold it in thine hand
I shall not die, but live, before thy face I stand
I for thou callest such, all that I have, I bring, all that I am, I give
Smile thou and I shall sing, but not question thy judgement much

Upon a gloomy night, with all my cares to loving flushed
Oh, venture of delight, with no one in sight
In safety, in darkness up the stairs I crept
O happy enterprise, concealed from others' eyes
When all the world in silence slept
Upon a beauteous night
I went without discerning and with no other light
Except that for which my heart was burning, it lit and led me through
More certain than the light of noonday clear
To thee who waited near, whose presence I knew well
O night, that was my guide
Oh, darkness dearer than the morning's pride
O night, that joined the lover
Transfiguring them each into the other
'tis that within my throbbing breast, which only for thee entire I save
Over ramparts fanned fresh winds fluttered
Lulled by airs which cedars wave
To my rest I sank, and all thy gifts thee gave
Until every sense suspended by thy caresses all my cares releasing

Lovers will always refer to themselves
But should not be loaded too much
With meanings from happier days
They must remain themselves, dear to the touch
The stars also must go on shining, knowing what we know
And the sunset must always glow
We two hath learnt the meaning all over again
The words, the sounds, our very touch
This time we must be firm, for we are new

The bough blossoms, the petals fall
Time makes no stir, though seasons run
Days lantern now, May is done
Prints leafy trees upon my boundary wall
And all the wealth that June bestows
Penurious winter will lay his pall
The golden apples will wizen all
And the heart dreads what the mind knows
Yet still, within the movement glows
In which all times and time are one
Where blooms the never-withering rose
And shines undimmed the immortal sun
New joys and gems his beams disclose
Time makes no stir, nor seasons run

The ocean, so it comes in, the moon trailing it
Does it not remind us two of many things?
Perhaps love most of all, the pull and thrust
And the gentle subsidence of the waves
To a clear, cool wash, of foam upon the sand
A sudden deafening stillness, but not for long
The waters seethe, a continual battling
Spiral, foam, and then the climax
Lasting a second, lasting a lifetime
Then moves on without need of human words or surrender
Yet satisfying our every sense, we feel, we love

Thou lingering star with lessening ray
That lovest to greet the morn
Again thou usher in the day
My lover from my soul was torn
Oh! Brenda dear absent shade
Where is thy place of blissful rest?
See thou thy lover lowly laid
Hearst thou the groans that rend his breast
That sacred hour can I forget?
Can I forget that hallowed grove?
Where by the winding lane we met
To live one day of parting love
Eternity will not efface
Those dear memories of love now past
Thy image of our last embrace
Ah, little thought of the world now past
Trent gurgling, kissing a pebbled shore
Overhung with wild woods of thickening green
The fragrant birch and hawthorn hoar
Twined amorous around this raptured scene
The flowers spring wanton to be pressed
The birds sang love on every spray
Till too, too soon the glowing west
Proclaimed the speed of winged day
Still o'er these scenes my memory wakes
And fondly broods with miserly care
Time but the impression stronger makes
As streams their channels deeper wear
My Brenda, my dear departed shade
Sweet thee thy lover lowly laid

Sleep softly in thy quiet bower, my dearest love
Let no mournful yesterday disturb thy peaceful rest
Nor let tomorrow concern thy waking thought
Only dreams of coming ecstasy
Thy Jonathan, thy changeless lover
His love surrounds thee, forget thyself and all the world
Put out each burning light, the stars of love
Are watching overhead, sleep softly then
Goodnight, my love

I sit looking out of this window
An ache within my breast
Smoke from 'Old Toms' garden fire
Drifting helplessly upwards
As dead leaves twirl and whirl
Hither, thither, downwards to earth
The tree which has its top chopped off
Stands now, stark and bare of life
Dreading the coming winter
Not knowing whether spring will come again
To its now lifeless branches
A blackbird shrieks in fear
As the Italian moggy leaps
How helpless that ice cream van looks
Thump, thump someone climbs the wooden stairs
Towards my quiet sanctuary
I am startled from my thoughts
Foolish, foolish me
I thought this would set me free

I must not think of thee, tired yet strong
I shun the thought that lucks in all delight
The thought of thee and heaven's delight, in the message of song
Oh! Just beyond the sweetest thoughts of thee
This breast, the thought of thee, waiting hidden yet bright
But it must never, never come in sight
I must stop short of thee the whole day long
But when sleep comes too close each difficult day
When night gives pause to the long watch I keep
And all my needs and bonds loosen apart
Must doff my will as raiment laid away

Then, and only then, when first dreams come with first sleep
I run, I run, I am gathered to thy heart
We are tenderly entwined
The mountains rise, desert winds howl
Oceans roar and rush
And yet, and yet dearer than my deathless soul
Still would I love thee, my dearest Stott Bush

It is a sweet thing to be loved by thee
Although my sighs in absence wake
Although my saddened heart is moved
I bear and smile for love's dear sake
My songs their wanton music make
Joyous and careless, songs of youth
Because the sacred lips of both are set always to kiss goodbye
Because my sweet glances weep for thee
That we must always part and love must die
Remembrance of love's long delights is to remember sighs and tears
Yet I always think upon the nights
I have whispered passionately in thy ears
The fond desires, sweet faint fears
My lover's limbs of lissom white
Gleam in the darkness with strange light
Thy wondrous orbs voluptuously
Bent on me all unearthly bright
Fond limbs with mine entwined
Thy hands gently caressing me
My ears grow deaf, my eyes grow blind
My tongue hot with thy kisses free
Short of madness, we lazily lolled back on our bed of fire
That I was weary, yet thy desire
Drew thee upon me, Brenda, my fire
Thee work thy pleasures until I tire
For thus did love's embraces wane
Though lusty limbs grow contentedly quiet
And our mouths' red valves are over fain, to suck the sweetness from the night

Amorously, with touches light, steal passion from reluctant pain
So as the day star flees again before the blushes of the sky
So I clasp thy knees in vain
Oh, thy sensuous lips, open to my kisses, thy hands playing with my hair
And find delight for me to bare, thy bosom, and passionate mound
White and for Venus's temple, round a garden of wild thyme whose eye
My sword of love shall pierce, yet shall not wound, oh, my Brenda, thy kiss
Shall linger on my palate still
No joy on earth is like this, that we have tasted our fill
For all our sweet lascivious will, the cup is drained of lust delight
I well with pleasure, and by night
I'll commence once more and moving lie
Between thy amorous limbs, despite that we must part and love must die
Thus, my dearest sweet, I'll sing when day doth break,
And weary lovers must awake
To part, but now our pleasure take, in one last bout of rivalry
Whose passions first shall answer a dance to make the curtains shake
Oh sweetheart, even if it were so, we could not speak, as words are cold
    and weak

Close together we lie, watching darkness slowly unfold
No clock counts the time when kisses are repeated our arms enfold
There is no telling where time is, only it is October
The leaves hang yellow and still, behind the eye a star
And under the quietness of this night,
All tell time, yet time is nowhere
We love, yet leaves have not timed this moment
No clock needs to tell us two, we have what we remember
Moments appear. Love goes on, this we share
And this we feel quietly like the trees casting their crowns
Into deep silent pools, without the peace of the surface being disturbed
And as an autumn leaf drifts to the ground
Gives the heart a wound or wakes an ancient grief
But let us not weep at all the leaves of autumn dies
Only weep that we should live to see them fall
Like birds flying through the empty air, crying as though from broken hearts
Made stiff with despair, and sighs like love that cannot reach love's eternity
So if thee love, pray forgive the weakness of my words

Brenda, why should we delay
Pleasures shorter than a day
Could we, (which we never can)
Stretch our lives beyond their span?
Beauty like a shadow flies
And our youth before us dies
Or would youth and beauty stay
Love hath wings, and will wisp away
Love hath swifter wings than time
Change in love to heaven doth climb
Gods that never change their state
Vary oft in love and hate
Brenda, to this truth we owe
All love betwixt us two
Let not thee and I enquire
What has been our past desire
On what shepherds thee hast smiled
On what nymphs I have beguiled
Leave it to the planets too
What hereafter we shall do
For the joys we now do prove
Let us dwell on present love
Brenda, let us live and love
Let crabbed age talk what it will
The sun goes down and returns above
But we, once dead, must be so still
Kiss me a thousand times, and then
Give me one hundred kisses more
And when this is done
That our pleasures may remain
We'll continue on our bliss
By unkissing them all again

This day returns, my despair burns
This blissful day we two did meet
Though summer wild in tempest toiled
Ne'er summer sun was half so sweet
As the ecstasy of love
Yes, heaven gave no more; it made thee mine
Whilst day and night can bring delight
Of nature's pleasures give
While joys above, my mind can move
For thee and thee alone I live
When the grim fate of life below
Comes between to part us
The iron hand that breaks the bone
It breaks my bliss, it breaks my heart

Why didst thou go, I wander still in these lanes
The light we sought is shining still
Does thou ask proof? Our sunset still crowns yonder hill
Bare on its lonely ridge, my love still lingers there
Thy voice in soft whispers often comes
To chase fatigue and fear away
Know him thy lover a wander still
Thou art gone, I, thee leave here
Alone in these lanes, yet I will not despair
Beneath the canopy of clear skies, and now the night
In ever-nearing circles weaves her shade
I see thy face draw soft across the sky
My heart bounds at emotions new
And hope once crushed is quick to spring anew
There is no other love but thine
I changeth not, nor will

For thee and love walk hand in hand alone the summer way
As thee pass, the world pauses for a little while
With gentle pace to listen to the song
Borne over the moonlit silvered Trent
Oh, youth and love, to have a springtime of your own
Far off and how incredible the time between now seems
My love, may it be long before thy gardens loses its summer hue
And when its leaves are brown
May spring dwell in thy heart, with all her dreams

Oh night, that joined the lovers
Transfiguring them into each other
That within my throbbing breast
Which for thee entire I save
Lulled by airs that cedars wave
I sank to my rest upon thee
And all thy gifts thee gave
Until every sense was suspended
By thy caresses, all my cares releasing
Thy neck I wounded unthinking
So rapt was I, so swept away
Lost to myself I stayed
My face upon my lover laid

This naked earth is warm with summer
Green grasses, trees, and flowers
Lean to the sun's glorying gaze
Life is colour, warmth, and light
Striving evermore for these
He is dead who cannot see
Or take warmth and light from this glowing earth
Day ends and night enfolds lovers in soft wings

Life had I loved the more
Had it passed away
As quietly and as passionately
Deep and raptured pain
Soothed like gentle rain
My wild tempestuous heart

I am at peace with all
A lonely impulse of delight
I find this tumult in the clouds
In balance, all brought to mind
A waste of breath the years behind
In balance this life, this death

I ask of thee neither external love nor fidelity
But simply truth, unlimited honesty
If my heart were brave enough to love
Without being loved
I would tear it to pieces

Love stings when it should tingle
And leaves scars instead of deep impressions
There is no warranty or bond to cover damage
No guarantee of finding love again
Perhaps giving over that one facet
Of yourself you held back last time

A candle in the thighs
Warms youth and seed and burns the seeds of age
Where no seed stirs
The fruit of man unwrinkled in the stars
Bright as a fig
Where no wax is, the candle shows its hairs
Light breaks where no sun shines

I did not feel the laughter in thy voice
Or feel thy arms entwine
Thy absence hurt somehow
Dull inside and out
I do not like this feeling very much
But I do not wish to be without it

I worry over thee, because I am part of thee
I worry for myself because I find
That I want nobody else but thee
Can I take care of thee
I need taking care of too
And from the look of things
There is no one else equipped but you
To move into this very much-lived life
But you

I do not run, but stand by my love of thee
I know not what lies beyond
Be it nothing or a new dawn
But with thee I shall rejoice
For my choice is with thee, my love

All through the night in my dreams will I keep
Soft visions of thee, as darkness enfolds
I wish more than ever, that thee could be here
To lie in my arms
And feel your touch
I want thee, my darling, I love thee so much
This feeling we share, such joy in a kiss
Thy lips on my lips
This love shall last beyond time

Awakening this morning after being loved by thee
The long fingers of the sun coming through the window
Picking out the dust, in the predawn hours
Lying together all arms and legs entwined
In this very narrow bed we lie head to head
And breath to breath
With the morning of departure coming too soon
And now thy face and the sun
Have made this room an avenue of sunlit dust

The folded, all-enclosed snow
That shrouded earth in a silent peace
Warned us two of what we would least know
How swiftly runs life's dwindling lease
The years that dim our memory
And fade the blooms of late lost hours
Still leaving the musing mind to see
A scatter of spring's early flowers
And late relenting time may pledge
The latest and loveliest spring
With blackbird in the hawthorn hedge
And the cuckoo calling on the wing

Now as tinted clouds cross the sun
Like so many golden-fleeced sheep
Winding their way wearily home, midst the dying day
My thoughts turn to our lane of happiness
The sun has crossed the sky
And was slowly sinking behind the patchwork of trees
A perfect circle of orange and gold
Rolling down the face of the day
And soon to fall into the dark wings of night
Too quelled with sorrow, to hold back a grief-laden tear
And we two, laced together with silver threads of love
Drift slowly softly, wherever the gentle breeze blows
A raindrop ran down the window
A silent crystals tear of joy and sadness, a most precious thing
And thee, a warm, most beautiful person
To keep out the cold of long winter's nights

When I woke up, it was Sunday
The birds were singing the night away
I saw my socks lying on the chair
Looked around but thee were not there
There were birds singing, trees blowing but no you
So I went downstairs, and dinner was fine
There was turkey and pudding and lots of wine
And I made small talk with a laughing face
Till my heart reminded me that you were not there
There were table and chairs, cups and saucers, but no you
Now it's almost Monday, and I hum a tune
It's nearly midnight, and I feel fine
Should old acquaintances be forgotten
There was music and dancing, whisky, and vodka
And sudden thoughts, all of them about you
So it's all the best for the year ahead
As I stagger upstairs and into bed
Then I look at the pillow by my side
I tell thee, Brenda, I nearly cried
There'll be spring, summer, autumn, and winter
All of these seasons without you

Take of me that which is my own
My love my life and my poem, the pain is mine and mine alone
See how the weight in bone, the hawk hangs perfect in mid air
The blood pays dear to raise it there, the moment not the bird divine
And see the peaceful trees extend, their myriad leaves in leisurely dance
They bear the weight of sky and cloud, upon the fountains of their veins
In the rose with petals soft as air, I bind for thee the tides and fires
The death that lives within the flower, oh, gladly, love for thee I bear

In June, the seed fell, when the month was new
Looking down thy valley
None but thee knew of it, where thee lay in lover's arms
For in the tree of thy veins, thee tended thy Jonathan
The red and ripening Adam of thy year
Thy spring will be late and human, trees still nude
Night when thy child came, thine own flesh
In the cry of a child, thee sit, not knowing
That this was a stranger, milk ran wild across the heaven
Imperiously he sipped off thy delicate beakers
Thee proffered him, thy little Jonathan
How were we to know that thee had corrected
The very tilt of this earth, on its new course

When thee are old and grey and full of sleep, nodding by the fire
Take out my letters from their hidden place and slowly read and dream
Of the soft look thy eyes once had, and of their shadows deep
Of how I loved thy glad moments of glad grace and loved thy beauty true
But ever did this guy love the pilgrim soul in thee
And loved the sorrows of thy changing face
Now bending down beside the glowing bars
Murmuring, a little sadly, of our love
Now fled above to pace the mountain overhead, lost amongst a crowd of stars

I wish thy beautiful breasts were brimful of milk
And that thee might nurture our child
Why possess two mounds in white skin—silk
When thee do not bear our infant child
To succour and feed on the seeds of our love
Must my passion be so wild?
Be described as wile and my futile guile
Conceptions are never created above,
So thee must give thy love the sign
Must my fire of desire be raised so much higher?
End in naught, but a funeral pyre
For thee woman to whom truth is known
It is by thy decree that our flesh not be free
In thy design only our minds must entwine
In our corporate life we find we share
That constant which pervades the sir
And the time is here to lay bare mutual care
So I'll dare to say what I believe is fair
Thy spirit will rest amongst God's best
But thy embodiment too shall be extended on
After thy frail body has departed, has gone
For thee top exist into progenitorial eternity
His is a vision that derides all my bestiality

How when I speed to thee sometimes in disbelief
To find thee waiting there at some rendezvous
Thy slender body seems to be a shaft of moonlight
Thee cast no shadow
Thy whisper of love is too soft for credence
Thy tread like blossoms drifting from a bough
Thy gentle touch upon my face, even softer
Thee, my love, with thy tender mask
Hiding all thy sorrow, grief, and concern
Which high on mountain tops in heather flow
Entrances lonely shepherds
All though a single word scatters all doubts
I quake for wonder at thy choice of me

Oh, Wild, Exciting James Jonathan Created by Brenda
Now my sleeping little boy
I will give thee a golden dream
My sleeping little joy
Saudi Arabia for thy morning
Egypt for thy noon
Europe for thy kingdom
Thee shall be its head
My sleeping little boy
My pretty sleeping joy

All the words I utter
All the words I may write
May they spread their wings untiring
And never rest is flight
Till they come where thy sad, sad heart is
And sing to thee in the long night
Beyond where troubled waters move
Storm darkened and starry night

Too proud to cry
Yet tears well within
I do not regret one moment
Spent with thee
Loving, fighting, or even hating
We two can never
Be otherwise not even in death
A tear is a gift from the Saviour

Written to James by his dad John Johnson

Skipping down the eggshell path
Of thy butterfly years
Yellow tendrils flying behind thee
Swept back by your delight
A flower about to open petal by petal
About to gladden this world
Yes, gather me a daisy chain of thee
Made from thy boundless joy
To wear in thy lover's winter
When the glow of snow
Pales to the far scent of fragile frost
Dearest Brenda of the cowslip and wildflower ways
Running deep across my October fields
Drowning me in pollen
Of thy madcap years
Making pain seem solace
All child and sudden wisdom
Just always amazing me

James

Slender golden-coloured hair
Joyful, energetic, and young
For thee are kindred to many things
The wild ducks' flight, swallows' wings
Autumn gold of trees
Swiftness of mountain streams
The magic of morning frost
Pureness of white driven snow
All has shaped thy dreams
Thee have a birthright no man can deny
A secret joy no man can tell

I hurried across the playing fields, I was coming home again
Thee was home, waiting for thy man
That short quick embrace, a long kiss, you looked wonderful, darling
In that moment, all troubled thoughts of remaining cold and aloof went
And as the morning enfolded itself about us two, like thy hair
Thousands of dispersed forces commenced to draw us together like a magnet
Light streamed through the windows even on a cloudy, rainy day
It seemed a million sunbeams poured through; what was destiny seeking
    in us two
What outlet, an immense vigour awoke within our bodies
Our souls expanded and overflowed into the day
And we, despite it all, were one again here and with all the world
Thy beauty shone into me like starlight and infused my passion
Thee were all female, ripe as a cherry and ready for plucking,
And I was male and could no longer resist thee and my need
The earth obeyed the rhythm of our movements
The house and trees sighed with us
Infinity was about to be emptied, to both of us it seemed
We two have never loved before; a miracle was in the air
And we knew that we two were not only accomplishing the act of love
But the whole universe throbbed with us two
And a great design was fulfilled
As our bodies bathed in each other's love, weak and trembling
And listening to thee breathing without an ounce of strength within
We two had gorged upon ecstasy, all consuming like an earthquake
Shutters down, like wind uprooting trees and spinning round
We fell at last, pleasure past, all anguish gone, is it death or life?
Brenda, awake from thy dream, laugh in thy innocent way
Thy countenance and light upon thine eyes is still as sweet as yesterday

This living darkness is to me
As thy dim, shadowed raven hair
And in my heart the thought of thee
Is as holy as a prayer
For to gaze into thine eyes
Or to touch thy hand
Stirs within me deeper mysteries
That I can understand
This, my love of thee is such
At thy lips so sweet
That other love I seem to touch
That filled the heart of Christ

Of Marriage

You were born together, and together you shall be evermore
You shall be together when the white wings of death scatter your days
Aye, you shall be together even in the silence of his nature
However, let there be spaces in your togetherness
And let the winds of heaven dance between you
Love one another, but do not make a bond of love
Let it rather be a moving sea between the shores of your souls
Fill each other's cup but drink not one cup
Sing and dance together and be joyous, but let each be alone
As the strings of a lute are alone
Though they quiver with the same music
Give your hearts, but not into each other's keeping
For only the hand of life contain your hearts
Stand together but not too near together
For the pillars of wisdom stand apart
And the oak tree and the elm tree grow not in each other's shadow
Your children are not your children
They are the sons and daughters of life's longing for itself
They come through you, yet they belong not to you
You may give them your love but not your thoughts
For they have their own thoughts
You may have housed their bodies but not their souls
For their souls dwell in the house of tomorrow
Which you cannot vista, not even in your dreams
You may strive to be like them
But seek not to make them liken to you
For life goes not backwards nor tarries with yesterday
You are the bows from which your children as living arrows are sent forth
The archer seeks the mark upon the path of the infinite
He bends you with all of his might that his arrows may go swift and far

Let your bending in the archers' hand be for gladness
For even as he loves the arrow that flies
So he loves also the bow that is stable
Their blood and your blood is naught
But the say that feed the tree of heaven
And when I crush thee to my body, say in your heart
Your seed will live in my body
And the buds of all your tomorrows will blossom in my heart
And your fragrance shall be my breath
And together we shall rejoice through all seasons
Your heart knows in silence the secret of days and nights
But your ears thirst for the sound of your heart knowledge
You would know in words that which you have known in thoughts
You would touch with your fingers the naked body of your dreams

The hidden wellspring of thy soul rise and run murmuring to the sea
But let there be no scales to weigh your unknown treasure
Seek not the depths of your knowledge
The treasure of thee is a sea, boundless and measureless
Say not 'I have found the truth', but rather 'I have found a truth.'
Say not 'I have found the path of my soul.'
Say, 'I have met my soul walking upon my path.'
For do not our souls walk upon all paths?
The soul unfolds itself, like a lotus of countless petals
We would know the secret of death
But how shall we find it, unless we seek it in the heart of life
The owl whose night eyes are blind unto the day
Cannot unveil the mystery of light
If we would indeed behold the spirit of death
Open your heart wide unto the body of life
For life and death are one
Even as the river and sea are one
In the depths are hopes and desires, lies our silent knowledge of the beyond
And like seeds of dreaming beneath the snow, our hearts dream of spring
Trust your dreams, for in them is hidden the gate of eternity
Our fear of death is but the trembling of our love
When standing naked before each other

The hand of God is laid upon us two in honour
For what it is to die, but to stand naked in the sun
And to be whispered away by the wind
And what is it to cease breathing
But to free yourself from life's restless tides
Only when we drink from the river of silence,
Shall we indeed sing
And when we reach the mountain top, shall we begin to climb
When the earth shall claim our limbs shall we truly dance
And the death may hide us, and a greater silence enfold us
Should my voice fade in thy ears,
And my love vanish in your memory
Then I will come again with a richer heart and lips more yielding
To thy spirit shall I speak and again seek your understanding
Yes, we will return to each; we will not seek in vain
If ought I have written is truth
That truth shall reveal itself clearer
In words more kin to thy thoughts
Know, therefore, that from a greater silence I shall return
In a little while, a moment of rest upon the wind
Then we shall be together again
No other woman shall know my love

Still may we meet again
And together build one house
Before we die
I love thee alone

Thine is the face that the earth turns me
Continuous beyond its human features lie
The mountains that rest against the sky
With thy eyes the reflecting rainbow the sun's light
Sees me, forest and flowers, bird and beast
Know and hold me forever in the world's thought
For when thine hand touches mine, it is the earth
That takes me, love's presence has no end

Above all shadows ride the sun
And stars forever dwell
I will not say the day is done
Nor will I ever bid thee farewell
Over death, over dread, over doom lifted
We live again unto a long glory
We will know again this sweet contentment

We walked hand in hand with love
Towards our future
In a morning that for all the world
Could have been
A day of tender spring
And did we not catch an echo within ourselves,
Soft and clear as faraway music?
That only the heart can hear
Music of a world
Where we are both young and in love
Or was it only a dream of a dream?

Make thine own magic
Do not let us say nothing beautiful comes our way

Here they stand two hundred cadets wearing poppies
To honour the dead in two glorious wars
Red for blood and rage and loyalty
Singing in sweet and well-washed voices
Of sacrifice, waste, and faith
Never to be forgotten as I stand
And sing the good old words myself
Not sweetly, but with a sound soiled by much use
With memory how appropriate I think
How sad in all the khaki uniforms
The cadets stand in ranks
God's little soldiers on parade

All destined as we were, or are they?
For battlefields and desolation
Already as I watch their fresh bright pink innocent faces
Praising those who fell
The eventide of horror rises within me
The darkness deepens, pity and pain abides
And all around me ghostly forms appear, ancient friends
The glorious dead wanting

Some days up ahead will be empty
Some years, fuller more loving
Than the fullest one we have known
This weekend has been quite full
I thought thee ought to know
That I thought it time to say thank you
For what has passed between us two
That in your mind thee may have felt
That thee missed my attention

Father now has eighty-six years
Of laughter, hunger, happiness, and tears
Three sons, three daughters proud
A one-woman man he would say quite loud
A shepherd's son, born to work
At twelve years old no thought to shirk
A boy soldier at sixteen
Close to men, immune from fear
After all those battles, mud, and grime
His medals lost in course of time
A lovely Scottish girl he wed
Out of trouble all of us she led
A gardener, flowers home he brought
And what we has was his support
Sometimes meat off his plate
When children we would wait

If walls could speak in that old home
The parties and weddings flowed
Sickness and comforts there bestowed
This spreading family have all joined
We'll remember father
And your independence that you'll keep
Newer dust upon this place is shed
We stand and see and never cry again
Under the primrose and bluebells he lies
The valley and mountain beneath his feet
Weds the eternal sunrise
Farewell, dear father
Thy memory will live on in the woods and flowers wild

Death of an Airman

I know that I shall meet my fate
Somewhere among the clouds above
Those I fight I do not hate
Those I guard I do not love
My country is St George's Cross
My countrymen Scotia poor
No likely end could bring them loss
Or leave them happier than before
Nor law, nor duty bade me fight
Nor public men, nor cheering crowds
A lonely impulse of delight
Drove me to this tumult in the clouds
I balance all, brought all to mind
The years to come seemed waste of breath
A waste of breath, the year behind
In balance my life this death

Silent—this world, its hushing long since complete
Where in the power of its stillness, thee are still asleep
And if thou ever didst hold me close to thy heart
Or in this harsh world draw breath in pain
Breathing like one that hast a weary dream
And suddenly feel a sudden calm so deep
Then know thee this we have but a short time to stay
Thee and I dry away as hours do, on a spring day
Like summer's rain or pearls of dew upon the morn
Our love, ne'er to be discovered again
Hearts that once heaved, now forever still